高等院校英语语言文学专

总主编 戴炜栋

Best American Flash Fiction of the 21st Century

21世纪美国微型小说选读

Tom Hazuka

Mark Budman

上海外语教育出版社
外教社 SHANGHAI FOREIGN LANGUAGE EDUCATION PRESS

图书在版编目(CIP)数据

21世纪美国微型小说选读/(美)哈祖卡(Hazuka, T.),
(美)布德曼(Budman, M.)编.—上海：上海外语教育
出版社,2007
(高等院校英语语言文学专业研究生系列教材)
ISBN 978-7-5446-0570-0

Ⅰ.2… Ⅱ.①哈…②布… Ⅲ.①英语—阅读教学—研
究生—教材② 小小说—作品集—美国—21世纪 Ⅳ.
H319.4：Ⅰ

中国版本图书馆 CIP 数据核字(2007)第 138253 号

出版发行：**上海外语教育出版社**
　　　　　（上海外国语大学内） 邮编：200083
电　　话：021-65425300（总机）
电子邮箱：bookinfo@sflep.com.cn
网　　址：http://www.sflep.com.cn　http://www.sflep.com
责任编辑：权　锋

印　　刷：上海外语教育出版社印刷厂
经　　销：新华书店上海发行所
开　　本：890×1240　1/32　印张5.5　字数185千字
版　　次：2007年11月第1版　2007年11月第1次印刷
印　　数：3 100 册

书　　号：ISBN 978-7-5446-0570-0 / Ⅰ・0022
定　　价：10.00 元

本版图书如有印装质量问题，可向本社调换

高等院校英语语言文学专业研究生系列教材

编委会主任：戴炜栋

编　委　（以姓氏笔划为序）

王守元　山东大学
王守仁　南京大学
冯庆华　上海外国语大学
石　坚　四川大学
庄智象　上海外国语大学
朱永生　复旦大学
何兆熊　上海外国语大学
吴古华　清华大学
杜瑞清　西安外国语学院
汪榕培　大连外国语学院
陈建平　广东外语外贸大学
周敬华　厦门大学
罗选民　清华大学
姚乃强　解放军外国语学院
胡文仲　北京外国语大学
贾玉新　哈尔滨工业大学
陶　洁　北京大学
黄国文　中山大学
程爱民　南京师范大学
戴炜栋　上海外国语大学

高等院校英语语言文学专业研究生系列教材

总 序

近年来,随着我国经济的飞速发展,社会对以研究生为主体的高层次人才的需求日益增长,我国英语语言文学专业的研究生教学规模也在不断扩大。各高校在研究生培养方面,形成了各自的特色,涌现出一批学科带头人,开设出自己的强项课程。但同时我们也认识到,要使研究生教育持续健康地发展,要培养学生创新思维能力和独立研究与应用能力,必须全面系统地加强基础理论与基本方法方面的训练。而要实现这一目标,就必须有一套符合我国国情的、系统正规的英语语言文学专业研究生主干教材。

基于这一认识,我们邀请了全国英语语言文学专业各研究领域中的知名专家学者,编写了这套《英语语言文学专业研究生系列教材》,旨在集各高校之所长,优势互补,形成合力,在教材建设方面,将我国英语语言文学专业的研究生培养工作推上一个新的台阶。我们希望通过这套教材的出版,来规范我国的英语语言文学专业的研究生课程,培养出更多基础扎实、知识面广、富有开拓精神、符合社会需要的高质量研究生。

在内容上,本套系列教材覆盖了英语语言文学专业各学科的主要课程。我们总的编写指导思想是:结合我国英语语言文学专业研究生教学的实际情况与需要,强调科学性、系统性、先进性和实用性。力求做到理论与应用相结合,介绍与研究相结合,中与外相结合,史与论相结合,广泛搜集资料,全面融会贯通,使每一本教材都能够反映出该研究领域的新理论、新方法和新成果。本套教材的这些特点,使其有别于单纯引进的国外同类原版教材,是国外教材所不可取代的,两者的作用是相辅相成的。也正是由于这些特点,本套教材不仅可以作为我国英语语言文学专业研究生的主干教材,也可作为中国语言文学专业的教师与学生的参考用书。

在编写体例上,我们参照了国家标准局的有关标准以及国际上的通行做法,制定了统一的规范。每章后面,都列出了思考题和深入阅读书目，以便启发学生思考和进一步深入研究。

　　教材建设是学科建设的一项重要基本建设，对学科发展有着深远的影响。我们相信，正如国外剑桥和牛津大学出版社出版的语言学和应用语言学教材和丛书对推动国际语言学和应用语言学的发展起了巨大作用一样，在世纪之交推出的这套系列教材，也必将大大推动我国21世纪英语语言文学专业研究生教育事业的发展，促进我国英语语言文学研究水平的提高。

戴炜栋
2000年9月

Introduction

By Mark Budman

Dear Chinese Reader,

    While it is true that every foreign language is difficult for a non-native speaker, there are ways to make the learning process easier for you. One of these ways is reading. We are talking about not just any text, but fine, literary fiction. For the beginner, this fiction should be short, satisfying and to the point. Flash fiction aims to provide exactly this experience, and we believe that you will find excellent examples of this type of reading in this book.

    So what is flash fiction? In his famous play *Hamlet*, William Shakespeare writes that, "Brevity is the soul of wit." Brevity. What a word pregnant with meaning! Yet brevity alone cannot be the answer; otherwise "I want food" or "Give me money" would be excellent examples of flash fiction.

    Flash fiction rests on what I call a tripod—plot, language and characters. And yes, it has to be brief. Think tabletop tripod and not the one a large telescope sits on. How brief? For the purposes of this book, 500 words or less. At this short length, the tripod has to be precise and the focus right on target. No wobbling, no mincing of words. Remove one leg of the tripod, and the story will collapse. And the publisher will turn away, or the reader will leave yawning. That's the worst punishment for a writer.

    Writing a memorable story in only 500 words is a challenge. We encourage you to practice, and to try to write flash fiction yourself. Like a sculptor with a block of stone, you must cut unnecessary words until you get to the very core of the story and your senses tell you that you can't cut any more. Yet at the same time, nothing important can be left out.

    Rich, literary fiction can never be completely understood, neither by writer nor editor nor reader. There are always various possible interpretations. That's

Introduction

why authors need intelligent readers to cooperate in the process of making sense of a text. That's why we need you.

What should you pay attention to when you read flash fiction? First, appreciate the author's ability to squeeze the essence of a situation into such a tight form. Notice the intricacy of language that is poetic yet also tells a story. Pay careful attention to every word, as if you were reading a poem, because in good flash fiction every word is important.

By accomplishing all of this, you will achieve a double victory. You will master the English language, and you will be introduced to a new genre of fiction.

As a starting point to your discussions, we have grouped the stories by theme: Death, Hate, Love, Fantasy, Foreign Lands, and War and Crime. These categories are designed to start you thinking, not to limit your interpretations. Many of these stories are complex and could have been placed in several different categories.

Happy learning, and may your path to the English language be both productive and pleasant.

Contents

Death

Sleeping   By Katharine Weber
.... 3 ....
The Dead   By Beverly Jackson
.... 6 ....
Clawd   By G. W. Cox
.... 9 ....
Indian Casino   By David Schuman
.... 12 ....
The Man with the Shovel
By Chauna Craig
.... 15 ....
Parting Ways
By Randall De Vallance
.... 18 ....

Hate

The Story of You   By Justine Musk
.... 23 ....
The Dark Side of the Moon
By Mark Budman
.... 26 ....

Homeward Bound   By Tom Hazuka
.... 29 ....
Argument for a Shotgun
By Dan Leone
.... 32 ....
Damn Irene   By Susan O'Neill
.... 35 ....
Black Silk   By Ian Randall Wilson
.... 39 ....

Love

All It Loves   By Avital Gad-Cykman
.... 45 ....
Headless Angel   By Tom Hazuka
.... 47 ....
La Guaca   By Daniel A. Olivas
.... 50 ....
Memento Mori   By Susan O'Neill
.... 53 ....
Infarction   By Kellie Wells
.... 56 ....
Buddha's Happy Family Jewels
By Vylar Kaftan
.... 59 ....

Contents

Sleep-over   By Bonnie Jo Campbell
.... 62 ....
7:23 PM   By Sherrie Flick
.... 65 ....
Exercise   By Bruce Taylor
.... 68 ....
Family Therapy   By Pamela Painter
.... 71 ....
A Room of Frozen Dust
By Marge Simon
.... 74 ....
Skins on Sule Skerry
By Sonya Taaffe
.... 77 ....
Beached   By Jessica Treat
.... 80 ....
Beer and Gunplay
By Neno Perrotta
.... 83 ....
The Illustrated Woman
By Pedro Ponce
.... 86 ....
Nebraska Men   By Sherrie Flick
.... 89 ....

Fantasy

And Counting   By Mark Budman
.... 95 ....
Snapdragons   By Alex Irvine
.... 97 ....
The Bookkeeper's Treasure

By Candi Chu
.... 100 ....
The House and the Homeowner
By Dan Leone
.... 102 ....
Rapture   By Gayle Brandeis
.... 105 ....
The Human Pyramid
By Neno J. Perrotta
.... 108 ....
The House Broods over Us
By Bruce Boston
.... 111 ....
The Curse of Fat Face
By Michael A. Arnzen
.... 114 ....
The Mouth   By Lincoln Michel
.... 117 ....
Wrong   By Aimee Bender
.... 120 ....
Centerfold   By John Briggs
.... 122 ....

Foreign Lands

Divadlo   By David Fromm
.... 127 ....
On Holiday   By Chauna Craig
.... 130 ....
Gatwick Blues   By Kay Sexton
.... 133 ....
The Lothario   By M. J. Rose
.... 136 ....

Contents    iii

What You Can Learn in a Bar
By Robert Reynolds
.... *139* ....
La Luna de los Tres Limones
By Steve Frederick
.... *143* ....

War and Crime

How Could a Mother?
By Bruce Holland Rogers
.... *149* ....
Three Soldiers
By Bruce Holland Rogers
.... *153* ....
Skin Deep
By Robert Boswell
.... *156* ....
No Questions Asked
By Patrick Weekes
.... *159* ....

Death

How do people cope with death and dying?

Is death the end of everything?

Can a human soul defeat death?

Death Sleeping

By Katharine Weber

She would not have to change a diaper, they said. In fact, she would not have to do anything at all. Mrs. Winter said that Charles would not wake while she and Mr. Winter were out at the movies. He was a very sound sleeper, she said. No need to have a bottle for him or anything. Before the Winters left they said absolutely please not to look in on the sleeping baby because the door squeaked too loudly.

Harriet had never held a baby, except for one brief moment, when she was about six, when Mrs. Antler next door had surprisingly bestowed on her the tight little bundle that was their new baby, Andrea. Harriet had sat very still and her arms had begun to ache from the tension by the time Mrs. Antler took back her baby. Andy was now a plump seven-year-old, older than Harriet had been when she held her that day.

After two hours of reading all of the boring mail piled neatly on a desk in the bedroom and looking through a depressing wedding album filled with photographs of dressed-up people in desperate need of orthodonture (Harriet had just ended two years in braces and was very conscious of malocclusion issues) while flipping channels on their television, Harriet turned the knob on the baby's door very tentatively, but it seemed locked. She didn't dare to turn the knob with more pressure because what if she made a noise and woke him and he started to cry?

She stood outside the door and tried to hear the sound of a baby breathing but she couldn't hear anything through the door but the sound of the occasional car that passed by on the street outside. She wondered what Charles looked like. She wasn't even sure how old he was. Why had she agreed to baby-sit when Mr. Winter approached her at the swim club? She had never seen him before, and it was flattering that he took her for being capable, as if just being a girl her age automatically qualified her as a baby-sitter.

By the time the Winters came home, Harriet had eaten most of the M & M's in the glass bowl on their coffee table: first all the blue ones, then the red ones, then all the green ones, and so on, leaving, in the end, only the yellow.

They gave her too much money and didn't ask her about anything. Mrs. Winter seemed to be waiting for her to leave before checking on the baby. Mr. Winter drove her home in silence. When they reached her house he said, My wife. He hesitated, then he said, You understand, don't you? and Harriet answered Yes without looking at him or being sure what they were talking about although she did really know what he was telling her and then she got out of his car and watched him drive away.

Questions for consideration

Does the baby really exist?

Why would Mrs. Winter hire a babysitter?

About the story

"Sleeping" is a story inspired by Katharine Weber's own inexplicable

Sleeping By Katharine Weber

teenage experience, minding a baby she never saw. It explores the mysteries of human desire and human behavior, and how difficult it is for people to truly understand those mysteries, even within themselves.

About the author

Katharine Weber is the author of four novels, and her short fiction has appeared in numerous publications including *The New Yorker*. A book critic and essayist as well, she has taught fiction writing at Yale University and elsewhere, although she herself has never completed a college degree.

Death

The Dead

By Beverly Jackson

We walk every morning, our pace well suited—old dog and old woman—a leash uniting us in silent journeys down country roads. The redwoods and Douglas firs creak in winter gusts that push us along. The sky is a changing panorama of purest pinks and the clear blues of newborns' eyes. Glorious enough to explain why people think heaven is skyward. The mist steams on a horizon of pines.

A dead mouse in the road is tiny, scrawny, with gray fur. If not for the black ooze beneath its head, it looks asleep. I drag Murphy away, his nose urged toward the scent. The following morning, we see a thin snake flattened on the pavement, its scales glittery in the early light. Its skin is unharmed, like a flower pressed under the wheels of a car or truck. As I again yank Murphy from the kill, I see movement—an infant is silhouetted, perched high in a tall, soft fir. It's a flash, an image. I cup my hand over my eyes, but she is gone—a mirage.

Next outing, bitter cold, the trudge up Arcadia Road is arduous. Murphy's fur ripples against his flanks in the wind. I wonder, for the millionth time, how different life might be, had the child been born. I shiver with cold and my dark thoughts. "Better take a quick whiz, Murphy," I say. The wind shakes the trees, making a whooshing eerie rustle. The dawn skies are flat and gray.

On the road an injured wren huddles, motionless. I hold Murphy back as I swoop it up. It struggles only a little. I move it gently to the grassy shoulder where it sits, immobile, while my mind battles between leaving it to survive in nature, or taking it home. Murphy's interest has been captured by a movement in the trees.

The baby appears again in the fir. No mistake. She is perched naked and rosy on an outer limb. The tight curls of her hair are honey-colored, and her face dimples with mirth as she waves her tiny fist.

It begins in my chest, and explodes in my ears, filling my mouth and nose. My head rings with the screech of wind and cries that must be born in my own constricted throat.

For years I've wondered what she'd look like, this child of mine. She gaily waves and I lift my hand in response, as if our fluttering fingers spin a thread, forever connecting us. She waits, I now know.

The vision of her fades in and out of the dappled foliage of the woods.

At my feet, the bird takes a few faltering steps, and I swipe my wet face with the sleeve of my parka. When I look back, the empty branches, heavy with needles, sway, waving.

The wren lifts off in a dazed and haphazard little circle. Then, buoyed by wind, it soars up into the trees.

Questions for consideration

Why is the sense of loss so important to the story?

What role does the dog play here?

About the story

"The Dead" is in the tradition of "magical realism" whereby ordinary circumstances are transformed into a magical scenario in order to exploit the emotional or psychological depths of a story. In this case, a woman is in the throes of her old age and the realities of death (for all creatures, some of which she finds dead or dying on the road), and most importantly, the loss of a baby in her past—the child she never had. Through imagery, the pain and loss in her life is manifested by a magical appearance of the unborn child in a tree—forgiving her mother and awaiting her too. The bird that she saves could be read symbolically as redemption of a sort. A reminder of the joy of living, the reality of the short span and finality of it all.

About the author

Beverly A. Jackson (former editor and publisher of INK POT and LIT POT PRESS, INC.) is a writer of poetry and short fiction. Her work has appeared in both print and online literary journals including *Vestal Review*, *Melic Review*, *Night Train*, *Zoetrope All-Story Extra*, *Absinthe Review*, *God Particle*, and *Rattle*, to name only a few. She is working on her first novel titled "The Loose Fish Chronicles."
http://www.beverlyajackson.com

… Death

Clawd

By G. W. Cox

My old man brought home a gift from Texas or Arizona. It beat the customary stick of Wrigley's Spearmint from his suit coat pocket. It was live. It was a praying mantis.

I named it Clawd. I watched him for hours. His spiky caliper arms swayed at guard like a sparring boxer. Behind them, his head gyrated, incessantly seeking prey. In tender moments his claws would snap onto my fingertip.

Unlike other insect pets, Clawd ate heartily. His favorite meal was grasshopper. Fine with me, coming home from school most days with grasshopper tobacco juice on my fingers.

Clawd would freeze curious with the grasshopper I'd caught. Then, *fwat*, he'd grab it at the top of the thorax and in the middle of the abdomen. His little mouth would gouge great chunks from the back, chomping away like me with corn on the cob. The grasshopper would struggle with half its back gone in an open brown wound.

Clawd lived in a sturdy shoebox in the basement. For his view and ventilation, I cut out parts of the box and replaced them with screen. For his exercise, I caught flies and let him flail away at them.

One day in late summer, Clawd refused to move. I nudged his arms and his whole body was stiff like a twig. I dropped to my knees for a closer look. His abdomen was flat as a small elm leaf. I moved some of the dead grass and saw an oval gray blob. Clawd had died from shitting his guts out.

I buried him in a velvet jeweler's box with a satin interior. I tied a cross with twine and two sticks. I stuck it in the ground where the lawn mower couldn't reach. His cage with the blob was chucked into the trash.

Years later I read a text with the facts of life for praying mantises. The female eats her mate during or just after making love. Months later the female lays the egg pod and dies. I stared at the close-up photo of the egg pod. It looked familiar. I should have named Clawd Clawdette.

I find solace knowing that in a dump warmed by the city's decomposing garbage, thousands of Clawdette's descendants roam free, hundreds of miles from their natural habitat. Eating a cornucopia of bugs. Breeding and dying with smiles on their faces, their arms clutched in eternal prayer.

Questions for consideration

Why is this insect so important to the boy?

Is the ending of this story optimistic?

About the story

"Clawd" claws its way into a boy's life as a gift from his father. The boy feeds the bug flies and grasshoppers, and the two bond through the simple clutch of a claw. Years after the bug's death, the boy realizes he is godfather of the spiritual life of the city dump. Inspiration and possibilities can be found in unlikely places.

About the author

G. W. Cox spent 26 years in newspaper work. Now he lives and writes in New Mexico with his wife, Magda, and pet, a dog.

Death Indian Casino

By David Schuman

My son wakes me in the middle of the night. This is unusual because he is a heavy sleeper—he once slept through a hailstorm that left pockmarks on the hood of the car and two crushed robins in the backyard.

"We need to go to the casino," he says. "I had a dream."

I mumble something about it being two-thirty in the morning but he is unimpressed.

"Mom was in the dream," he says, and hands me my pants.

His mother, my wife, has been dead for a year and three months.

The river takes an hour to get to, and there's the casino, garish against a dingy dawn sky. Beyond the flashing lights, a barge glides past on the river. I have read about pleasure boats that get too close to the barges, underestimating their speed. It is all over for them.

"She said you had to play the slots. She was sort of singing it," he says, pressing silver dollars into my hand, one by one, until there's a little column of them in my palm.

"This isn't tooth fairy money?" I ask. The look that he gives me could remove paint from a wall.

"Say her name when you pull the lever," he says.

I leave him three stories up in the garage, parked behind a pillar of concrete as thick as a redwood. I tell him to keep the doors locked, against who I'm not sure, but a casino parking lot is no place for a boy.

Indian Casino   By David Schuman

A few days before she died, I saw my wife push my son's hair out of his eyes as he lay with her in the hospital bed. "Be good, little onion," she said. I order his favorite pepperoni pizzas instead of making meatloaf and vegetables, I take him to science fiction movies that his friends' parents won't let them see, and I bought him a parakeet who shits on my shoulders, but "little onion" is the thing he is going to remember as long as he lives.

There are more people in the casino than I thought would be here this early. The carpet has a pattern of tomahawks, but I don't think Indians have anything to do with this place. The gamblers carry jumbo plastic soda cups with tokens inside.

You expect me to say that I came out of there with nothing, but that is not what happened. When I open the car door, my son is roused from sleep. The pattern from the upholstery is impressed on his cheek.

"Did we get lucky?" he says.

For the first time I have something to tell him.

Questions for consideration

What is the importance of the casino to the plot?

How do the father and son bond together?

About the story

"Indian Casino" is a story about a father dealing with the death of his wife and a son dealing with the death of his mother. It's about the family they've become since she died, and how they navigate their grief. The casino, with its flashing lights and promises, is a beacon to them in some way. The father and son are drawn to it in the middle of the night. We don't know exactly what's happened in the end, but the events of the story may help them communicate with each other directly rather than through dreams and memories of a woman who is no longer there.

About the author

David Schuman teaches fiction writing at Washington University in St. Louis where he is also Assistant Director of the graduate writing program. His fiction has been published in numerous literary journals including *Conjunctions*, *Missouri Review* and *Black Warrior Review*. He is the executive editor of *Land-Grant College Review*, a literary magazine based in New York City.

Death

The Man with the Shovel

By Chauna Craig

The man with the shovel dreamed once of the trapeze. He was a boy then. He'd gone to the circus with his father, a man who would leave. The air flashed bright with red leotards, bodies flipping through space. Someone always caught these bodies with slender hands, slight fingers that could miss or snap off like twigs. But first came the breathless moment, the what if.

What did you like best?

The man who would leave was still there then, driving fast in the dark as the boy slumped under his seatbelt. His stomach cramped with cotton candy and warm lemonade. The seatbelt pinched and pulled. He said, the flying people.

You mean the acrobats? People can't fly.

And he nodded, yes, the acrobats who lived on air.

The man with the shovel is too slow for the one who drives the orange public works truck. He moves slower as the day grows long. The driver honks and swears. *They're fuckin' animals. They're fuckin' dead. They don't need last rites.*

The man with the shovel never explains. He scrapes the squirrels from suburban drives, gently balancing them as he steps towards the truck. He knows they've been hit by things they couldn't outrun. Some are flattened, bloody pelts.

But so many of the bodies he lifts are soft and whole. He pretends

Death

their toes missed a branch, that a tiny twig gave. Maybe their hearts burst from the altitude. Yes, he thinks when he sees no blood, burst hearts.

He launches them from the end of his shovel. They flip in the air, white bellies flashing through sunlight. Flying squirrels. *People can't fly*. Squirrels limp as those acrobat bodies in the moments before they were caught. Late in the day, when the truck bed is full, lined with feathers and fur and the odors of decay, he knows they land safe.

The man with the shovel dreamed once of the trapeze. He was a boy then. When the driver backs in and raises the end, broken bodies slide into the pit that yawns like a mouth. Fur and feathers collapse. Squirrels and birds and the cats that chased them, nestled now in eternal truce.

The man with the shovel waits near the piled earth. All is still, except the delirious flies. All is muted and dirt-dulled but the guts. They shine red, bright leotards stripped inside out.

Question for consideration

Can the power of dreams change one's life?

About the story

"The Man with the Shovel" is a story about the human dream of transcending our mortal limitations. The boy who wanted to believe that people could fly becomes the man who, through his imagination, transforms the dead animals on the roadside into something beautiful—

acrobats performing their art. When he "launches them from the end of his shovel," they become something more than ordinary roadkill, even if only in his own mind. That is the power of art—to help us see beyond the obvious to all the possibilities for beauty in this life.

About the author

Chauna Craig is a professor of creative writing at Indiana University of Pennsylvania. Her stories have appeared in numerous literary magazines and anthologies, including *Sudden Stories: A Mammoth Anthology of Minuscule Fiction*. Her work has also been cited in *Best American Essays* and *The Pushcart Prize Anthology*.

Death

Parting Ways

By Randall De Vallance

There was the death, of course, and the funeral and a week later, Marianne visited the grave for the first time. She took along a small bouquet of roses, white ones, and laid them on the grass in front of the headstone. Knowing she needed this time alone, I waited by the car and smoked a cigarette. I fully admit that I was indifferent to her plight, but I had no desire to upset her further, and so kept myself at a distance where I would not have to become involved.

The person who died I did not know. But to Marianne it was someone important, which I guess made her important to me. It was sunny and cold, and a breeze made Marianne's long, blonde hair swirl and dance like the clouds of smoke I pushed from my lips. It was the only thing distinguishing her from one of the monuments: she stood perfectly erect, head bowed, hands clasped in front of her waist. Dressed all in black—the heels and the stockings, the peacoat and beret—she seemed only more pale.

An hour passed that way, but I was not impatient with her. The cemetery was not unappealing to me: aesthetically, I had the deepest appreciation for it. The exactness of the monuments, the obvious care that went into their making, from the grandest mausoleum to the most modest grave marker, spoke of a sincerity that had seemingly disappeared from our lives. It had retreated here, to a place where cynicism could never intrude, where the source of all our dread and

Parting Ways   By Randall De Vallance

bitter joys was memorialized, spreading out beyond the edge of sight, in every direction, to a place my eyes could not reach.

When the sun had fallen lower, filtered gold through the bows of the oak trees that dotted the grounds, I summoned the courage to speak Marianne's name. But she made no answer, and I could see then that she was already too far gone, that no matter what I said or how I pleaded, she was simply not ready to leave. Perhaps she would never be ready. Coming up behind her, I leaned in and kissed her one last time on the cheek. Her eyes remained fixed on the headstone as I got in the car and drove away, leaving her to recede in the rearview mirror.

Questions for consideration

Did the story take place at the funeral?

Who died?

About the story

"Parting Ways" is centered around the oft-repeated idea of life as "a series of beginnings and endings", or "births and deaths". With only five hundred words to work with, flash fiction is better suited to symbolism and the conveyance of impressions than plot and character development. In this case, the event—the funeral—is of course symbolic of the dissolution of the narrator's relationship, the nature of which is never discussed. Likewise, the circumstances that led the relationship to go wrong are never stated; no answers are sought in this case and no blame is assigned to either party. This vagueness is intentional, and serves to show that all things—just like life itself—have an end, and acceptance of that fact is often the only way forward.

About the author

Randall De Vallance is a 2002 graduate of Edinboro University. Over twenty of his short stories have appeared in such publications as *Eyeshot*, *Opium Magazine*, *Vestal Review*, and *Pindeldyboz*, and have earned him a Pushcart nomination and a place on StorySouth's "Notable Stories of 2004" list. His first novel, "Dive," was published in 2004 by Exquisite Cadaver Press and is available online at Amazon, Barnes & Noble, and all other major book retailers. Currently he is serving with the Peace Corps in Zemen, Bulgaria.

Hate

Why is hate such a strong emotion?

How can you control your hate?

Is hate justified sometimes?

Hate

The Story of You

By Justine Musk

You were lean and dark-haired in your open-air Jeep. You made your left turn and I followed, all the way to the cafe on South Beverly Drive. I took a corner table, drank a mocha latte, watched you flirt with the redhead. Guys came up, asked for a seat and a chance. I licked foam off my lips. I only wanted you.

Weeks passed, and I learned you so well. You approached me in the club, said, "How come we don't know each other?" We squeezed onto the dance floor. I put my mouth to the warm salty hollow between neck and shoulder, moved my tongue along your skin until I found your pulse.

That was my first taste of you.

You never learned me at all. "She's a sweet girl," I heard you say on the phone. "She would never do anything like that." That was your version, which begins, we met at a club, and ends, I'm in love with Lucinda. I'm sorry. I hope we'll be friends.

But it began at the corner of Wilshire and Beverly Glen, your wild swing into a reckless left.

The heft of the gun in my purse. The way to your house through this maze of sun-slammed streets.

I am the one telling the story, my love.

I will be your ending.

Hate

Questions for consideration

What item in the woman's purse tells us about danger?

What might happen in the end?

About the story

Every story has more than one side, especially the story of a relationship. "The Story of You" is about who gets to control the story of one particular relationship. The man thinks the truth is very simple: he met the woman at a club, she is "a sweet girl" and their relationship is over when he rejects her for another woman.
What he doesn't know is that the woman has been stalking him ever since she first saw him in his car, when he was making "a wild turn into a reckless left". She is not a "sweet girl": she has a much more malevolent character. When he betrays her, she refuses to let him be the one who decides how their story will end. So she waits for him with a gun in her purse. She will be the one to have the final say—"I will be your ending"— and her version of their relationship will be the one that matters most.

About the author

Justine Musk was born in 1972 in a small town in Ontario, Canada. She went to Queen's University and graduated with a first-class degree in

English literature. After living and working in Australia and Japan, she moved to California. She is the author of three dark-fantasy novels, *Bloodangel* (Roc/Penguin), which was published in October 2005, and *Slayer of Angels* (Roc/Penguin) and *Stranger* (MTV Books/Simon & Schuster), which will be published in 2007. She lives in Los Angeles with her husband, young sons, and dogs.

Hate

The Dark Side of the Moon

By Mark Budman

When I was six, I waded into the Black Sea until the water reached my cute belly button. I asked my father, "What's on other side?"

"Bulgaria," he said. That sounded mealy, like an arid bagel.

"And after that?"

"Western Europe."

I knew what a Western was—a movie where they ride horses and fight Indians.

"And after that?"

"The Atlantic ocean."

"And behind the ocean?"

"America."

I knew Americans wore top hats, smoked cigars, exploited workers and wanted to bomb everybody, especially my Motherland. But I didn't know they were that far.

"What is closer, America or the moon?"

"Spanking," my dad said with his usual half-smile. "That's the closest thing to you." He thought for a second and added, "Violence determines conciseness."

I didn't know he was making a Russian language pun on the Marxist maxim "Environment determines conciseness."

Many years later, I stood at the New Jersey shore and watched clouds eat the pale moon by the Eastern horizon. The cell phone rang.

"It's better be good," I said.
"It's done, boss," was the reply.

I hung up and stuck my cigar back into my mouth. If you blow the whistle in my company, you won't last long.

Questions for consideration

How does the reality of life change the person?

What kind of man is the protagonist now?

About the story

"The Dark Side of the Moon" tells a fable about a young boy who grew up in Russia fantasizing about America. It seemed as unknown to him as the dark side of the moon. Yet when he grew up, he immigrated to the land of his dreams and became a ruthless American capitalist, the type he used to fear.

About the author

Mark Budman's fiction, creative non-fiction and poetry have appeared or are scheduled to appear in such literary magazines as *Mississippi Review*, *Virginia Quarterly*, *Exquisite Corpse*, *Iowa Review*, *McSweeney's*, *Cafe Irreal*, *Another Chicago*, *The Bloomsbury Review*, *The Cincinnati Review* and *Night Train*. *Exquisite Corpse* nominated him for the XXVI Pushcart Prize. He is the publisher of a flash fiction magazine *Vestal Review*, http://www.vestalreview.net, and the recipient of the Broome Country Art Council grant. One of his stories has been accepted for the new WW Norton anthology "Flash Fiction Forward."

Homeward Bound

By Tom Hazuka

Thanksgiving, 1970, changing planes at a Midwestern airport. I wasn't feeling thankful, not even for my sky-high draft lottery number. I felt more guilty than good about luck shielding me from decisions I'd never wish on anybody: Canada, prison, Vietnam.

A soldier in a wheelchair was smoking Luckies like his life depended on it. He had a newspaper on his lap but wasn't reading it; I saw ashes on the headlines. After awhile two soldiers sat in front of me, discussing the football game. One hoped the storm would hold off because he hated God-damn turbulence.

A guy and a girl my age—college—came up to the wheelchair. "Vietnam?" he asked.

The soldier nodded.

"Good," she said. "Paralyzed, babyburner? Still got your manhood?"

"Yeah," he said, too quick, so quick it made you wonder.

The bigger soldier jumped up, but the skinny one shoved him aside. He dropped the guy with one punch, then smacked the girl twice in the face.

A black security guard my father's age ran over. "Did you *see* that?" the girl shrieked.

"I saw it." He yanked the guy to his feet. "Now *get* outta here."

His voice was so venomous they fled without speaking. The wheelchair soldier was shaking, pretending to read the paper. The other

Hate

two sat down again, careful, like they weren't sure the seats fit any more.

"Sorry, man," said the skinny one, his voice full of holes. "I was afraid you couldn't do it."

I remembered going to Niagara Falls as a kid, the disappointment of crossing into Canada and not feeling any different on foreign soil. It was like the world was just all one place.

We took off late in the snowstorm.

Question for consideration

Why doesn't the security guard help the college guy and the girl?

About the story

"Homeward Bound" takes place during the Vietnam War. The American people were divided: many supported the war, but many others did not. Some Americans were so angry about the war that they blamed U. S. soldiers. That's what happens in "Homeward Bound," when two young people confront the soldier who has been wounded and is in a wheelchair. The problem is that they let their frustrations get in the way of human decency. No matter what your beliefs, you should not treat another person the way they treat the soldier. The two young people hate the violence of the war, but do not understand that what they say to the soldier is also a form of violence. Ironically, the words of the war protestors just lead to more violence—against them, this time.

Homeward Bound By Tom Hazuka

About the author

Tom Hazuka has published over 30 short stories and two novels, *The Road to the Island,* and *In the City of the Disappeared*. A former co-editor of *Quarterly West* magazine, he has co-edited two popular short story anthologies, *Flash Fiction* and *A Celestial Omnibus: Short Fiction on Faith*. He has co-written a book on college basketball, *A Method to March Madness: An Insider's Look at the Final Four*, and is currently a professor of English at Central Connecticut State University.

Hate

Argument for a Shotgun

By Dan Leone

You wake up in the middle of the night afraid of what? For me it's dead chickens, no more eggs and a bloodless bloody mess to clean. Weasels'll wipe out a whole houseload of chickens in one night, only knocking off the heads and sucking out the brains. For example.

For example I dream a fox with wire cutters and a crow bar.

"Where are you going?" asks my wife.

"Bathroom," I say.

"Why are you putting on your hat? Why are you putting on your shoes?"

"Go back to sleep," I say.

In the bathroom I open the window and stick my head all the way out into northern California, middle of the night. I think I hear a scratching sound coming from the vicinity of the chicken house. Bobcat, I think, trying to dig its way under the fence.

I need a shotgun. I really should have a shotgun, I think, running outside to meet the enemy with a curling iron and a toilet bowl brush.

The enemy, this time, is fog, condensing into water droplets on oak tree leaves and dripping onto other oak tree leaves, dripping down all the way eventually into the dead, crispy stuff I never rake around the chicken run. I stand there under the tree in the dark until my eyes adjust to no bobcats, no foxes, no hungry eyes or glistening teeth; just fog, just watery particles of atmosphere, the *is* of what *isn't*,

Argument for a Shotgun By Dan Leone

suspended like berries all around me—visible only because up there somewhere there's a moon.

I stand where I am until my heart rate returns to normal. Then I brandish the toilet bowl brush, stab at the fog with the curling iron, and head back inside.

"What was it?" my wife asks.

"Nothing," I say.

Questions for consideration

Why does the protagonist need a shotgun?

Why doesn't he tell his wife about his feelings?

About the story

"Argument for a Shotgun" is a story about fear. Dan Leone keeps chickens and loves chickens, for pets and for food, and since he doesn't have children, chickens are what's dear to him. And they're so vulnerable and defenseless, and so scared all the time. Rightfully so. They just taste too good to too many different animals, the author included. To raise chickens is to introduce a very real element of terror into one's life, and Dan Leone loves it. Because terror is going to be there anyway. This way it takes more concrete form. You have to protect the chickens!

So for a long time, at first, all he dreamed about was chickens and predators. He started not sleeping so soundly, jumping up in the middle of the night, same as before, only now he knew why, and this seems better to him. Even if there's really nothing out there. The fog, "the *is* of what *isn't*," as he put it, represents the idea that fear in itself is very real, founded or not. In fact, the fog, an empty dark night, a drop of water on a leaf, might be more dangerous than a fox, for example, since it renders shotguns and curling irons and other ridiculous weapons absurd.

About the author

Dan Leone writes a weekly humorous column about food and life for the *San Francisco Bay Guardian*. Leone has published two books, *The Meaning of Lunch* (Mammoth Press), and *Eat This, San Francisco* (Sasquatch), as well as numerous stories in literary magazines and anthologies.

Hate

Damn Irene

By Susan O'Neill

Harry dipped his paddle blade, the handle at chest level as Toni the Leader had taught them. Just beyond the three kayaks crouched a damp roll of fog; if he reached out, he could've grabbed a handful.

"We'll make for Burnt Island," Toni called. "It's getting murky—stick together, we won't get lost."

"Okay," Harry shouted. In the rear seat, Irene said nothing. He glanced back; she paddled clumsily, her face expressionless above her life vest. A wave tossed up spray. He shivered. Cold; he'd hate to have to swim in this bay.

"Left," Toni called. "Follow me."

Harry leaned into the paddle, dipping, dipping, but the kayak did not turn. Fog tickled his arm. "Left, Irene," he ordered. "Push the left pedal."

Behind him, her meek voice: "I can't, honey. It's stuck. The rudder won't go left."

"You're not trying," he said through clenched teeth. Damn Irene. She never tried. She'd seemed so eager to please last year when they were dating. Then he'd married her.

What a mistake.

She never complained, per se. But when he tried to teach her tennis—coached her, drilled, cajoled, rewarded, bullied, shamed her—she refused to hit the ball right. At last, he joined a club and left her to putter in her silly garden.

He bought her a bike. She didn't bother to keep up with him, and still she strained her knee.

Golf? She lost the balls. Camping? She got poison ivy. And when he took her hunting, she tripped and nearly shot him ("Oops; sorry, honey," she'd said).

Ron and Marcie's kayak shimmered off to the left and dissolved in the mist. Marcie, now—*there* was a game woman. Damn Irene. "Push your left pedal. *Push.*"

"I am, honey."

His neck hairs bristled. "You're not."

"I told you, the right pedal works"—He heard the rustle of the spray skirt that stretched from her waist to the rim of her compartment; the kayak lumbered rightward—"but not the left."

"Irene, straighten us out," he commanded.

"I can't, honey. Honest. My left pedal's broke."

Her wimpy tone set his teeth on edge. "Damn, Irene." He twisted, heard the dip-dip of her paddle, but she was lost in fog. "Turn this kayak left. *Now.*"

Silence.

Then, softly, tentatively: "Turn it yourself." Dip-dip. "Honey."

His eyes widened. Far away, a buoy gonged.

He slammed the paddle down on the fiberglass hull. "What'd you say?" His heart hammered. He jutted his jaw. "*What?* I'll be damned if I'll paddle for two."

"This wasn't my idea." Her disembodied voice sounded surprised: "You know, it's never my idea."

He heard the snap of a spray skirt pulling free. A splash. A gasp—*Whoo!* The kayak bucked, rolled over; grey water grabbed up for him. Cold. He heard arm-strokes, surprisingly strong, receding, fading, gone. His face bobbed under, up; his paddle knocked the hull, dodged his shivering fingers, floated away.

Damn Irene By Susan O'Neill

"Damn, Irene!" Up; under. "*Ireeeb?!?*"
But there was only the far-off gong of the buoy.

Questions for consideration

What kind of person is the man in the kayak?

What happened to Irene?

About the story

In "Damn Irene," a pompous and insensitive man is in a kayak group with his wife, just off the coast of the state of Maine. The woman, Irene, is in charge of turning the kayak with the foot pedals. One of the pedals is broken; when her husband refuses to believe her, she rebels against him in the only way she can, in a boat in the middle of the bay. The story is written in the man's point of view, and shows us how he sees her, and how he interprets her lack of skill or passion for the things he likes to do. Irene is a quiet character who tries to be what her husband wants her to be; it is only there, in the kayak, that she understands this is impossible.

About the author

Susan O'Neill   lives in Massachusetts with her husband. She writes fiction and non-fiction, has been nominated twice for the Pushcart Prize and has been named as a notable author by Best American Essays. She has published a book of stories based on her year as an Army nurse during the war in Viet Nam (Don't Mean Nothing: Short Stories of Viet Nam, published by Ballantine, 2001; Black Swan [UK], 2002; and UMass Press, 2004). She is currently looking for a publisher for a novel entitled "American Family". Her website is: http://susanoneill.us.

Black Silk

By Ian Randall Wilson

We lasted ten minutes at the restaurant. Silver earrings. Alcove. Her hand on me under the table. The crushed strawberries did it, juice running down that luscious throat.

She started undressing in the car, her dark skin luminous. She drew off her black silk stockings and flicked them. She kept her legs open, showing herself off to me.

At my place, we ran for the apartment door. Three steps inside, she wrestled me down, panting, tearing at my clothes. Ripped my shirt and trouser buttons getting them off. Then she was on top and grinding.

"Hit me," she said, out of nowhere. "Hit me hard."

On the rough carpet, in the darkness, I was falling. She rocked harder; sweat trailed down the cleft between her breasts. She hunched further, pulled my hand to her face.

"Hit me. *Please.*"

And I did. Once, twice, then a third time—in the face. Left the imprint of my fingers on her dusky-colored cheek.

It gave her what she needed. She went rigid, then collapsed to the floor. Rolling to her side, she started crying.

I spent a long time in the bathroom, washing my hands. She knocked, kept knocking.

"Jeffrey, I have to talk to you," she said.

Eventually she went away.

I never called. All that remains is a pair of black silk stockings folded in a drawer. Sometimes, when the light is gray or the night more empty than usual, I take them out. Then, I trace their crooked seams.

Question for consideration

Did Jeffrey love the woman in black silk stockings?

About the story

Even a student for whom English is a second language can easily understand the action of "Black Silk". Here is an American couple whose relationship is deeply troubled. The woman is more of a different race than the narrator which comes across in the reference to her "dusky-colored cheek." Other cultures may read this as a story of sexual indulgence that moves into depravity. Where is the line, though, in human experience, between normal and depraved? No doubt the story crosses it. And yet the narrator longs for the object of his obsession as we see in the final paragraph. The story is full of anecdotes until that paragraph. Here is one of the problems of this very short micro-fiction form. The challenge is to make the story into something more than mere anecdote. It is the last paragraph that does it. It is in the last paragraph that we come to understand how affected the narrator was by this single experience, and how he returns to it over time, over the years, to reexperience it: his dip into depravity, his humiliation, his loss. Many things in our lives trigger memories that bring up strong feelings about past experiences. The hope of the story is that it will resonate beyond the surface of its own telling to make the reader remember something he or she returns to with the same strength and depth of reaction.

About the author

Ian Randall Wilson's short stories and poetry have appeared in many journals including *The Gettysburg Review*, *The Alaska Quarterly Review*, and *The North American Review*. A faculty member at the UCLA Extension, he is the winner of the 1994 Cera Foundation Poetry Award. His first fiction collection, "Hunger and Other Stories," was published by Hollyridge Press (www.hollyridgepress.com).

Love

Which is stronger, love or death?

How do we know when we fall in love?

What kinds of love are there?

Love

All It Loves

By Avital Gad-Cykman

It is dawn, but the sun is still lying on the floor at the top of the stairs. Last night, I thought I heard a woman in a long dress coming up to kiss me goodnight: Mother. But it was the sound of the sun's petal brushing against the stairs, fluttering over the handrail.

I had made the bed, white crispy sheets, a soft pillow, a feathery blanket. However, the sun could not make it to the room. It dropped on the floor, exhausted, an enormous yellow chrysanthemum picked, smelled and thrown.

Now it is dawn, and I am looking up. The room next to mine is closed and silent. Mother's translucent face shutting eyes between white sheets. Outside, the darkness retreats to its shelter, and a pale light, the leftover of yesterday's summer, drifts uncertain in the air. It enters through our cracked-open door and peers at the sun.

I tickle one yellow leaf and then another; I pull at the third but straighten it with regret. The sun opens an eye and takes in the hesitant light, the visitor. It enfolds the light with care and lets it breathe for another moment of dawn. I stand against the goose-bumped wall and watch the sun open up, letting go of the light it has nurtured, releasing all it loves.

Questions for consideration

Is the mother in the story still alive?

What is the significance of the leaf in the story?

About the story

Once, the author saw a drawing of a flower lying at the top of a staircase. It reminded him of the sun, the way children draw it. The thought about children and the sense of light and dying beauty reminded him of a mother who died young, forced to release the embrace of her child.

About the author

Avital Gad-Cykman lives and writes in Brazil. Her writings have been published in *Glimmer Train*, *McSweeney's*, *Prism International*, *Other Voices*, *Happy*, *Stand Magazine*, *Stumbling* and *Raging Anthology* (McAdam/Cage,) as well as online in *Salon*, *Zoetrope All-story Extra*, *Salt Hill Review*, *3am*, *In-Posse Review*, and elsewhere.

Love

Headless Angel

By Tom Hazuka

Beth was three months pregnant when we went to France on our honeymoon. The trip represented our promise not to let the baby change who we were, not to forget that there was so much world, all around, waiting. Then in Normandy, strolling down to the beach for lunch, we saw a woman dive from a fourth-floor window and die on the sidewalk, right across the street. It was horrible, a shock out of nowhere on a gorgeous sunny day. People ran to the rag-doll body, yelling for a doctor, yelling for the police. But it was hopeless. Beth trembled against me in a way she never had before; I knew she was remembering her younger sister who had killed herself. Hugging each other hard, Beth and I walked to the shore. Young men in tiny bathing suits played volleyball on the sand, oblivious to what had happened two hundred feet away.

"It'll be all right," I said finally, to both of us. I put the untouched bread and cheese in my backpack, though I was very hungry. I squinted against the glare off the Atlantic. The water was cold here, all year round.

"Right," Beth said.

The next day we drove the abbey road, along the Seine. The river flowed slow and perfect in the morning mist. We stopped at the Abbaye de Jumièges and paid to enter the magnificent ruin, roofless walls and white stone spires reaching for the sky.

Beth disappeared.

I found her in a courtyard staring at a decapitated marble angel, its childlike hands palm-to-palm in prayer, the front of its bare feet broken off and worn as smooth as a windowsill polished by generations of elbows.

Beth touched the angel's wings. "Vacation's almost over, lover," she whispered. "Soon we have to fly home."

Our fingers intertwined on the cold, hard stone.

Questions for consideration

What is the significance of the suicide in the story?

Why is the statue of the angel headless?

About the story

"Headless Angel" is a story about life and death and the passing of time. Beth is pregnant, soon to bring a new life into the world. Death interrupts their happiness when she and her husband see a woman kill herself. This situation brings up the past, for Beth's sister also committed suicide.

The rest of the story contrasts the life of the two people in the present with the remnants of what people have done long ago. The beautiful building and the angel are now broken. The man and woman know that human life is short, and they hold hands. At least for now, they have each other.

About the author

Tom Hazuka has published over 30 short stories and two novels, *The Road to the Island*, and *In the City of the Disappeared*. A former co-editor of *Quarterly West* magazine, he has co-edited two popular short story anthologies, *Flash Fiction* and *A Celestial Omnibus: Short Fiction on Faith*. He has co-written a book on college basketball, *A Method to March Madness: An Insider's Look at the Final Four*, and is currently a professor of English at Central Connecticut State University.

Love

La Guaca

By Daniel A. Olivas

There was a man who owned the finest restaurant in the village. Though no name adorned the establishment, the villagers dubbed it La Guaca, the tomb. The man, as well, had no name, at least none that the villagers knew. He was a complete mystery, a man apparently with no family, no origin, no history. They called him El Huérfano, the orphan.

One evening, as the villagers gorged themselves on enchiladas, tamales and other delectable dishes, El Huérfano rose from his usual seat at the corner table and cleared his throat. The room fell into silence.

"I plan to take a bride," said El Huérfano to the startled villagers. "But,". he cautioned with a raised, elegant finger, "she must be perfect in every way."

Most of the families had at least one unmarried daughter because the Revolution had taken from this earth most of the village's eligible young men. So, this announcement raised great hope in the hearts of the parents and their daughters. "I invite all of the village's señoritas to feast here tomorrow night," said El Huérfano. "No one else may come. And I will choose my wife from among the guests."

"How will you choose?" an older woman asked. But El Huérfano turned and disappeared through a back door. A great cheer filled the void because this mysterious but wealthy man would make someone's perfect daughter a bride.

The next evening, all of the village's single women swarmed La

Guaca dressed in all their finery. Though El Huérfano was not the handsomest of men, times were hard and there was little chance of living a comfortable life without a marriage of convenience. Remarkably, all of the women found seats in La Guaca and they waited. The tables sighed with great platters of food and bottles of fine brandy. Finally, after what seemed an eternity, El Huérfano appeared.

"As you know," he began, "I search for the perfect wife."

The room murmured in anticipation.

"Before you sits a great feast," he continued, noticing one particular beauty who sat motionless amidst the others. "But it is poisoned."

A horrified gasp rose from the young women.

"The poison is so potent, it will kill in a matter of minutes." El Huérfano now whispered, "But it will not harm a perfect woman. If you wish to leave, please do. Otherwise, enjoy your dinner."

Only one woman stood and left. The others slowly served themselves and commenced eating, each believing that she would survive. After a few minutes, the first victim fell. And then there was another and yet another. Finally, only the most beautiful woman was left. She stood and walked to him.

"You shall be my wife," he said as he moved his lips to hers.

She leaned forward and they kissed. El Huérfano could taste the wonderful feast from the beauty's lips. But then his eyes bulged and he fell back.

"No!" he sputtered as he dropped to the floor.

"Yes, my love," said the beautiful woman. "Yes."

Questions for consideration

Why does the man die?

Is his death justified?

About the story

"La Guaca" is a dark variant of the classic Cinderella story where a prince saves a wretched but beautiful young woman from a life of toil and abuse. In this version, there's no prince, only a nameless man of wealth who is willing to poison many women to find the one "perfect" wife. His plan, of course, backfires, leading to his death by the very same poison that uncovers the perfect woman.

About the author

Daniel A. Olivas is the author of *Devil Talk: Stories* (Bilingual Press, 2004), *Assumption and Other Stories* (Bilingual Press, 2003), *The Courtship of María Rivera Peña: A Novella* (Silver Lake Publishing, 2000), and a children's book, *Benjamin and the Word / Benjamin y la palabra* (Arte Público Press, 2005). His writings have appeared in several anthologies and many publications including the *Los Angeles Times, El Paso Times, MacGuffin, Exquisite Corpse, Tu Ciudad, Vestal Review,* and *The Jewish Journal*. He is currently editing "Latinos in Lotus Land: An Anthology of Contemporary Southern California Literature," to be published by Bilingual Press in 2007. His web page is: www.danielolivas.com.

Love

Memento Mori

By Susan O'Neill

The baby was born with a hole in her spine, and all the love that Estelle and Art poured into it was not enough to seal her tiny soul inside. Estelle—daughter of Florida, tall, thin and elegant—chain-smoked cigarettes in a silver holder and clung to Art's broad chest. She swallowed her grief, buried it in her vacant womb, polished it to a fist-sized pearl with unshed tears. A year later, it thrust itself into the surgeon's hand, leaving her barren.

I was born then, Art's sister's first girl. Baby-simple, I warmed to my aunt's caresses, not knowing I had stolen them.

Estelle and Art lived exotic in the brick jungle of Chicago, while I tended cows and schoolbooks. I saw them little. But in my tenth summer, they drove me with them to Florida. My mother said, "You have always been her favorite."

I cared nothing for the Why. Wild with ocean, shoes leaking sand, I body-surfed breakers and gobbled crayfish, and gaped as Estelle's tiny mother dipped snuff from a jeweled snap-top box. I filled my Brownie camera with wonders: segregated beaches, motels. Tobacco fields. Lookout Mountain. Art and Estelle; her regal poise; his frayed black stogies. Leaning on the Buick. His broad hand brown on her lady-white shoulders.

Her bobbed black hair against his muscled arm.

Summer died. I stumbled fiercely about the barn, kicking chickens, stabbing cows with truculent stares.

Love

For Art, winter brought death. Mother told me one wind-whipped school afternoon: his heart.

I felt loss. But I was selfishly young, filled with books and plans and, yes, the dreaded cows. Estelle pulled Art's old Buick up to the snowbound house. Her head high, she drew me to her narrow smoky bosom, laid a scarlet-tipped finger on my cheek and searched my eyes—for what, I did not know. Then she nodded and drove away. To replant herself in Florida, with her mother.

I grew away, fast-forwarding from farm and family, grew like Jack's beanstalk through clouds into a blue sky of airplanes, into far-flung agoras and feluccas and minarets and yurts. I fell in love in a jungle, far from cows; we shimmered with life and purpose and made perfect children.

In Florida, a past land, Estelle's mother shrank and faded away. I sent the obligatory letter; I received pictures—Estelle tall, pole-thin, rail-straight, long cigarette held split-fingered at her chin, now minus the holder. Alone. Old. In her new Buick. Her letter spoke, strangely, of Art: Ah, I miss the man. He knew me.

She was eighty when her smoke-brittled bones crumbled. Estelle was gone, drifted ash, before I reached Florida. Side by side, my mother and I boxed away chic size-two dresses for charity in her haunted, orderly house.

In a bedroom redolent of pine and old smoke, buried deep beneath sweaters and lavender sachet, I found a small snow-white box.

Inside, cradled lovingly in rose-dotted tissue, lay hand-knit pink baby booties.

Questions for consideration

What kind of relationship exists between the girl and her aunt?

Memento Mori By Susan O'Neill

Why does the reader need to be reminded of death?

About the story

A girl who grows up on a farm in the Midwest tells about her elegant aunt, who once took her to Florida when the girl was a child. The story is about a secret sorrow the aunt carries through her life, and about the fact that the girl never discovers this heartache until her aunt died. The Latin words Memento Mori mean "a reminder of death."

About the author

Susan O'Neill lives in Massachusetts with her husband. She writes fiction and non-fiction, has been nominated twice for the Pushcart Prize and has been named as a notable author by Best American Essays. She has published a book of stories based on her experience as an Army nurse during the war in Vietnam (*Don't Mean Nothing: Short Stories of Viet Nam*, published by Ballantine, 2001; Black Swan [UK], 2002; and UMass Press, 2004). She is currently looking for a publisher for a novel entitled "American Family". Her website is: http://susanoneill.us.

Love Infarction

By Kellie Wells

I'm sitting on the nubby gold and brown brocade couch that chafes my legs in the summer, watching Red Skelton with my mother, cross-eyed Clem Kadiddlehopper capering pleadingly before the camera, which is where I first learned that people enjoy good-natured ignorance, look to it for reassurance that they are wise, make reasoned and discerning judgments (something that has always made me feel sad and extraneous), and I become suddenly and acutely aware of my heart beating, drumming madly, a percussive warning that the enemy approaches (I look at my chest to see if the insistent thumps are lifting my shirt), and I begin to think that it is only this awareness, now that the wire has been tripped, that will keep me alive, that I now have the burden of being constantly mindful of every beat lest, unremarked, this willful muscle ceases to contract altogether, and I'll fall to the ground, limp as a dish towel, victim of my own distractible nature, another lost child who failed to recognize God when He came knocking at her body's door. God is always muscling His way into my veins and joints, and, like the good flagellant, I thank him for my pain, but this is an ambush, boring into my preoccupied heart as I sit before the snowy Motorola, and I am determined to be worthy of it. I can tell as it hammers against my chest, a prisoner demanding release, that my God-infested heart will use any excuse to escape, any pretext to leap from my chest and beat a path toward the door. It is a test. This causes me to inhale sharply, and my mother turns to me, still grinning from watching Clem's antics, and it's clear that she sees the stricken

look creasing my face, though I try to conceal my terror. But she is accustomed to these looks by now—in fact, they became such a frequent occurrence that she took me to Dr. Yulich to see if this was normal, so many unsettling sources of panic and dread in an eight-year-old girl—so she strokes my cheek and turns back toward the television, just as Dr. Yulich advised. Meanwhile my heart seems to have dislocated itself, pulled free of the tethers that keep it from sneaking off to somewhere else in my body, stowing away in one of its many hidden compartments, and I frantically finger my sternum, try to hold the crafty heart in place, and then I feel my lungs inflating with air, flaccid balloons that fill and empty with my shallow breathing, something *else* I must now monitor, and I gasp, paw at my throat, sit forward on the couch, plant my feet on the floor, straighten my back. I turn to see my mother smile woodenly at the television, through the commercial, hands clasped in her lap, trying not to notice the mad child, the one who aches to be pure, arteries clogged with God, drowning in the body beside her.

Questions for consideration

Is the child in this story religious?

What is the significance of the sentence structure here?

About the story

"Infarction" is about a child whose obsessive and fretful search for God in the world results in a fixation on her own body. The child becomes almost cripplingly self-aware, fearful that if she's not, God will escape her and she will be doomed, fallen and impure. The long, circus-train sentences are meant, syntactically, rhythmically, to enact her fear, and connote, in their breathless momentum, her anxiety.

About the author

Kellie Wells was awarded the Flannery O'Connor Award and the Great Lakes Colleges Association New Writers' Award for her collection of short fiction, "Compression Scars." She is also a recipient of the Rona Jaffe Foundation Writer's Award for emerging women writers. Her work has appeared in various journals, including *The Kenyon Review, The Gettysburg Review,* and *Prairie Schooner*. Her novel "Skin" was published in 2006 by the University of Nebraska Press, in their "Flyover Fiction Series", edited by Ron Hansen. She teaches in The Writing Program at Washington University, in St. Louis.

Love

Buddha's Happy Family Jewels

By Vylar Kaftan

Jackie says, "Chinese food is supposed to mix together on the plate." I know him as Dave but he says he is Jackie. We are sitting in a bad-good Chinese place that uses quality grease. The centerpiece is a ripped silk flower and a wooden Buddha. The lunch in front of me has become orangecashew beefpork despite my efforts to separate it.

"I don't like it mixed up," I say. "I wish these plates had compartments."

Jackie shrugs. "It doesn't matter. It runs together anyway." He picks up the Buddha and strokes it thoughtfully. "His stomach is so smooth. And his head. No hair anywhere."

"I bet he has hairy testicles."

"I don't know if he has any at all," says Jackie.

"I've never patted the Buddha below the belt, but I think he does."

He hands me the figure. "I always thought the big belly was supposed to imitate early Goddess carvings. The miracle of life. Being a man would have been hard for him. I bet he tucks."

I rub the Buddha's belly. He feels reassuringly masculine. "I'm still sick in the mornings. We should have met for dinner instead. Or after the baby is born."

Jackie frowns. "Are you worried I won't give child support? I will, after I pay for the surgery."

"I don't care about the money," I say, setting the Buddha down. "I'd rather have you come home."

Now Jackie picks up the Buddha and studies it carefully. "I'm sorry, but I can't. It's not you, I swear. It's all me."

"I still love you."

Jackie sighs. "You never knew me. And that was my fault." He takes ten bucks and a tube of lipstick out of his purse. He puts the money on the table and freshens his lipstick. He smacks his lips in my direction, in a kiss that's not meant for me. He stands up and glides out the door, his high heels clattering on the tiled floor.

Questions for consideration

Is Jackie still a man?

What is the role of Buddha in this story?

About the story

Life is simpler when people can put everything into categories, but it doesn't always work. "Buddha's Happy Family Jewels" is about the blurring of boundaries. Every part of the story involves things mixing together: food, religion, even gender. The title itself is two phrases, blurred: two dishes mixed together to create something new. Even if people want to, they can't keep parts of their lives on different sides of the plate. Two notes that will help the reader: "Jackie" is a name for either a woman or a man, and "family jewels" is slang for testicles.

Buddha's Happy Family Jewels   By Vylar Kaftan

About the author

Vylar Kaftan's work has appeared in *Strange Horizons*, *Lenox Avenue*, and *Raven Electrick*. She attended Clarion West in 2004, and currently volunteers as a mentor for young writers through the Absynthe Muse program. Visit her website at www.vylarkaftan.net.

Sleep-over

By Bonnie Jo Campbell

Ed and I were making out by candlelight on the couch. Pammy was in my bedroom with Ed's brother; she wanted to be in the dark because her face was broke out.

"We were wishing your head could be on Pammy's body," Ed said. "You two together would make the perfect girl."

I took it as a compliment—unlike Pammy I was flat chested. Ed kissed my mouth, throat, collarbone; he pressed his pelvis into mine. The full moon over the driveway reminded me of a single headlamp or a giant eyeball. Ed's tongue was in my ear when Mom's car lights hit the picture window. Ed slid to the floor and whistled for his brother who crawled from the bedroom on hands and knees. They scurried out the screen door into the backyard and hopped the fence. Pammy and I fixed our clothes and hurriedly dealt a hand of Michigan rummy by candlelight.

"You girls are going to ruin your eyes," Mom said, switching on the table lamp. When Mom went to change her clothes, Pammy whispered that she'd let Ed's brother go into her pants. Her hair was messed up, so I smoothed it behind her ear.

"Too bad this isn't in color," Pammy said later, when we were watching Frankenstein. While the doctor was still cobbling together body parts, Pammy fell asleep with her small pretty feet on my lap. I stayed awake, though, and saw the men from the town band together

Sleep-over   By Bonnie Jo Campbell

and kill the monster.

Questions for consideration

Are the girls in the story ready to become adults?

What is the importance of Frankenstein in the story?

About the story

In "Sleep-over," two girls, about thirteen years old, are fooling around with boys while the adults are absent. A boy attempts to compliment the narrator, and tells her she is pretty by telling her that her head deserves to be on a well-developed body; this suggests how a man or a boy sometimes thinks of female body parts (such as breasts) as objects apart from the person to whom they belong. After the excitement of the evening has settled down, the narrator is watching an old Frankenstein movie and she realizes a scary connection between what the boy suggested doing to her and what the famous doctor did to create the monster Frankenstein.

About the author

Bonnie Jo Campbell is the author of the novel "Q Road," and the award-winning collection "Women & Other Animals." Her work explores the lives of women and girls in rural Michigan. She has won the AWP award for short fiction and a Pushcart prize, and she was named a Barnes & Noble Great New Writer. Visit her website at www.bonniejocampbell.com.

Love

7:23 PM

By Sherrie Flick

Paint your nails. Inhale. Exhale slowly. Let the paint dry.

It's easy. This waiting.

Once the nails are dry, do the dishes. Slowly, deliberately. Dry each plate, each cup, each bowl. Close each cabinet door without letting it make a noise. Inhale.

Vacuum straight lines in the carpet. Dust with the kind of precision your mother would be proud of. Exhale.

Think, think, think.

Check the machine for messages. When the solid red light is still solid and red, put your hands on your hips. Look up. Keep looking. Stand that way until your whole life clings to itself and settles at the base of your spine.

Take a shower. Exhale.

Look at yourself in the mirror. Suck in your stomach. Stick it out as far as it will go. Get dressed.

Imagine the phone will ring the minute you make yourself rush out the door.

Rush out the door.

As you walk to the bus stop, recreate the message word for word. It ends with love and a soft click.

Wait for your bus. Look up the street and down. See hope in the stoplight, the car alarm, the corner deli's lighted sign. Watch the bus

come screaming in.
    Let it leave the curb without you. Let it pull away.
    Squint. Raise your hand to your eyes.
    Wait for the next and the next and the next.

Questions for consideration

Does the sequence of commands work in this story?

What images do they bring?

About the story

In "7:23 PM," Sherrie Flick captures a complex emotional state without saying the words "sad" or "confused." So instead, she depicts quiet, tense repetitive movements. In the story, the woman is going forward with her life, but she is also pushing against an overwhelming force of hopelessness:
    "Imagine the phone will ring the minute you make yourself rush out the door.
    Rush out the door.
    As you walk to the bus stop, recreate the message word for word.
    It ends with love and a soft click."
Chances are the phone isn't going to ring, and if it does, there won't be a message about love on the answering machine when she returns. Instead, the character is only wishing this will happen; she is imagining a better scenario for her life—one that she isn't living right now.

7:23 PM   By Sherrie Flick

In this flash fiction, Flick uses short, clipped sentences as a means to reflect the character's hopelessness, even as she searches in vain for hope in all that she sees around her: the stoplight, the car alarm, the corner deli's neon sign.

Flick has written in second person "you" in order to make the scene more universal, to put the reader directly into the state of mind of the character.

About the author

Sherrie Flick   is author of the award-winning flash fiction chapbook "I Call This Flirting" (Flume Press, 2004). Numerous literary journals have published her work, including *North American Review, Prairie Schooner, Puerto del Sol,* and *Quick Fiction*. Anthologies include "Sudden Fiction: The Mammoth Book of Minuscule Fiction" (Mammoth Press, 2003), "Flash Fiction Forward" (W.W. Norton, 2006), and "New Sudden Fiction" (W. W. Norton, 2006). She lives in Pittsburgh, Pennsylvania where she is co-founder and artistic director of the Gist Street Reading Series (www.giststreet.org).

Love Exercise

By Bruce Taylor

Take a story from real life, one you are having trouble focusing. Cut the story in half. Cut it in half again. What you're left with is the essentials of the story you will be able to see more clearly.
(259 words)

They have said nothing to each other for weeks except what matters to the day, the children, the budget or the dog. He is upstairs at his office window. She is reading in a chaise longue in the shade some book her recently widowed mother gave her. She sighs, he imagines, at how it was an easy mistake for a young girl to make, a less likely error, perhaps, for a man so much older.

Who remembers mostly a white dress, a waist your hands could fit around, the scent of Juicy-Fruit and Noxzema. When he asks what's wrong, she always says she's happy; the only thing is, if he were sometimes a little happier a little more often too . . .

What she thinks of him now he doesn't even know, but fears it's so much less than what she thought at first, when he was what he can't imagine now, and obviously isn't to her now, and why and why? In the grief of his fifties, hard liquor sits him down to pray.

They treat each other as tenderly at least as they'd treat a relative or friend, a needy stranger or the obligatory guest. Whatever it is they might be discussing escapes to the underside of the birch leaves in the gathering breeze. The lights across the river are brighter and seem more

distant than the stars. The swallows give way to the bats and a tiny spider spins at the ruined screen a web someone less desperate might be tempted to take as a metaphor.
(130 words)

They have said nothing to each other for weeks except what matters to the day, the children, the budget or the dog. He is upstairs at his office window. She sighs, he imagines, at where love has led her and how it was an easy mistake for young girl to make.

He remembers a white dress, a waist your hands could fit around, the scent of Juicy-Fruit and Noxzema—he wants to ask her what she remembers.

They treat each other as tenderly at least as they'd treat a relative or friend, a needy stranger or the obligatory guest. Whatever it is they might be discussing escapes to the underside of the birch leaves. The lights across the river are brighter and seem more distant than the stars.
(64 words)

They have said nothing to each other for weeks except what matters to the day. She sighs at where love has led her. He remembers a white dress. They treat each other as they'd treat a stranger. Whatever they might be discussing escapes to the underside of the birch leaves. The lights across the river are brighter and more distant than the stars.

Questions for consideration

Is the same plot common to each of the mini-stories/chapters inside the longer story?

What did the author need to sacrifice in each consecutive mini-story?

Love

Who is the narrator here?

About the story

Most writing is addition, adding one word to another. This exercise asks you to do just the opposite. Keep taking things away, subtracting, until only the core of the story remains. It is like a sculpture stepping forward from the stone it was carved from. Here's an exercise for the reader, cut the last version in half again, and again?

About the author

Bruce Taylor's poetry, fiction and translations have appeared in such places as *The Chicago Review, The Exquisite Corpse, Light, The Nation, Nerve, The New York Quarterly, Poetry, The Vestal Review* and *E2ink-1: the Best of the Online Journals 2002*. His current project is a short fiction series called "Story Is" of which this selection is a part.

Love

Family Therapy

By Pamela Painter

Gathered together in her office, we are a mysterious centrifugal force dispersed around the bland interior. Earlier, each of us had a separate session of our own. Now, the therapist sits in our circle, trying for eye contact to reassure us that she is with us for the long haul.

To be here, my husband needed to inform his secretary to hold this time open, to arrange a continuance on the Haythorpe case, to leave work without a bulging briefcase that keeps him in our downstairs study past my bedtime, preparing briefs and citing precedent past midnight most nights, lights blazing.

To be here, our daughter had to deign to emerge from her bedroom whose canopied bed is hung with mosquito netting she refuses to discuss, emerge from behind dark glasses, from under headphones, arms crossed over a Marilyn Manson T-shirt, one of thirty on the floor.

To be here, our son was subjected to another fatherly, lawyerly outburst no longer effective, although my husband hasn't figured this out yet, so I threatened cancellation of the DSL line, and the withdrawal of help with college applications scattered around his bedroom where he sleeps beside his monitor, all lights on.

To be here, I needed to make the appointments, write my husband a reminder, watch my daughter write the time and place on the palm of her hand, and stick a post-it on my son's computer. I needed to leave my rosewood desk where I write my weekly column on new restaurants, to forego meditation, to leave my book on the guest room bed, where I frequently sleep or daydream of the ghost who wanders through the house, long skirts swishing against hard-edged Danish furniture, lantern held yearningly high in her search for something or someone. I needed to entice the family to assemble, cajole us to arrive today at the same time to hear just where we go from here.

But first, the therapist says, she has one other thing to say. Then she laughs, a tinkly laugh she surely would have stifled had she realized how dismissive she sounds about the only thing she could have said to send us out of her office forever, not cured—cured of what, anyway?—but a family again.

Giggling, my daughter rises to announce, "That settles that." Her brother follows her out the door asking, "Was it pearly white?" and then their father stands and looks around as if precedent has somehow failed him, but he'll give it another chance. He follows the kids, calling, "Let's all go to lunch." The therapist is clearly feeling left out, but what can I do but eventually pay her bill? As I gleefully join my family, I replay what the therapist said, moments ago, when we were still gathered in her circle, before we became a family again, hysterical with complicity and relief.

She said, "Before we begin, I want each of you to know: you have all seen the ghost."

Question for consideration

Will the family get together as a result of the therapy?

Family Therapy By Pamela Painter

About the story

"Family Therapy" is the story of a family that is estranged from each other because each person is keeping their own encounter with the ghost in their house a secret. The therapist is amused by this and considers her revelation that they have all seen the ghost a starting point to family therapy—but instead it is the "cure."

About the author

Pamela Painter is the author of the award-winning story collection, "Getting to Know the Weather," and of a recent collection titled "The Long and Short of It." She is also the co-author of the widely-used textbook, "What If? Writing Exercises for Fiction Writers." Her stories have appeared in *The Atlantic, Harper's, Kenyon Review, Mid-American Review, Ploughshares, Quick Fiction,* and *Night Train*, among others and in numerous anthologies. Two stories continue to be heard on WGBH's "Morning Stories." Painter has received grants from The Massachusetts Artists Foundation and the National Endowment of the Arts, has won three Pushcart Prizes and *Agni Review's* The John Cheever Award for Fiction. She is a founding editor of *StoryQuarterly*. Her story, "Reading in His Wake," first published in *Ploughshares*, and winner of a Pushcart Prize, was recently recorded for a W. W. Norton CD titled "Love Hurts." Painter serves on the advisory boards of Grub Street, RoseMetal Press, and Castle Hill. She lives in Boston and teaches in the Writing, Literature and Publishing Program at Emerson College.

Love

A Room of Frozen Dust

By Marge Simon

I meet you in Scarborough. The station is packed with passengers waiting for the next train south. Day by day, the ice is creeping over the earth, unimpeded by the swollen sea. It has obliterated whole cities. Across the channel, it encroaches on the highest peaks. Soon it will join glaciers.

I've booked the last room in the hotel still open to visitors. In the hallway two maids are finishing their work. One ducks her head as we pass. The other stares. "She's rude," I whisper, putting my arm around your shoulders.

Your eyes walk straight through me, avoiding the part that hurts. My hands tremble and the key is difficult. Someone has stripped the room. The telephone has been disconnected. At least the sheets are clean. We cover the window with my leather coat. We do not talk about the advancing wall of ice.

There is a candle on the dresser. You light the long wick so the flame burns high. It's hottest at the top, you say, and hold my hand over it, laughing when I pull away.

You tell me how your dreams are mashed up inside. Fix me, say your fingers when they come to free my belt. Your hair is pale moonlight. I touch it with a whisper, "Nothing is irrevocable."

Your dusky roses died, all bitterroot and weed. When I touch your thigh, you close your eyes.

A Room of Frozen Dust   By Marge Simon

I wake to a room of frozen dust, a blurred note by the telephone. It is a long way back to the station. I walk past the docks, where all is a shifting curtain of mist. The boats are ghosts on an anthracite sea. Ice spiders come with the fog. They spin pale webs over the street lamps, lambent rainbows on frosted glass.

I wonder if you fear the cold. If you feel it.

Questions for consideration

How does the cold affect the relationship in this story?

Is this story optimistic or pessimistic?

About the story

"A Room of Frozen Dust" is set in a world experiencing extreme climatic change. As the glaciers advance from the north, two lovers meet for a final night together. Their relationship is already estranged, a reflection of what they are going through in coming to terms with the new realities of their world. Their bodies and emotions become inseparable from the cold that surrounds them.

About the author

Marge Ballif Simon   free-lances as a writer-poet-illustrator for genre and mainstream publications such as *The Pedestal Magazine, Strange Horizons, Flashquake, Aeon, Flash Me Magazine, Dreams & Nightmares, From the Asylum* and *Vestal Review*. Her self illustrated poetry collection, "Artist of Antithesis", was nominated for a Bram Stoker award in 2004. Marge is former president of the Science Fiction Poetry Association and now serves as editor of *Star*Line*. Website: http://hometown.aol.com/margsimon.

Love

Skins on Sule Skerry

By Sonya Taaffe

When first they met, he stole her skin: cheaper than a wedding ring and twice as clear. All the soft storm greys, marbled silver and watered white silk, her throat, her thighs, the arch of her spine bundled away and collecting dust, became the secret kept at the crux of their hearts. There is a closet in the attic she does not touch. There are words they do not speak. Love is possession, the old word for this act committed between sheets with no smell of the sea on them; sometimes she tastes her tears and imagines the rising tide slipping against her mouth, his insistent rhythm the buffeting waves; he wants to know why she always keeps her eyes closed. So he has her, and has her somewhere in the house: her heart and her shadow, her soul and her self, the tidal core of her longing. When he is away at work, she wanders the house alone. A stranger looks back from the mirror's glass.

In the lonely afternoons, she writes laments for the grey salt gulf that was her home. She is not much of a poet. But he does not read them; fear averts his eyes. Lately the earth itself has begun to pull at her, soil crusting the soles of her feet, his seed a stone in her belly; she would sink, land-gravid, if ever the waves rose and spilled about her again. She pictures a blind fish, floating in the saline dark, and envies it. Tides come and go deep within her. The roar of the blood-sea sounds in its ears that cannot yet hear. Her child: his child: tightening the knot never tied at the altar, spurious claim on her substance. Her palms are bleeding from the clench of her fingernails. In the attic somewhere, no one sees the silver dip and shine of light on her fur.

Clumsily, he caresses her swelling flesh and says he loves her. Will it have her eyes, depth-dark? Her hair, the color of rain? He will love it because it is hers. He will never lose her. He knows how she feels. His language rattles like pebbles in her mouth, sparse, dry, skinned of meaning; she cannot answer him. Instead she spits in the dust at his feet. In the mornings, nausea like sea-sickness grips her. She rises unsteadily, one hand on the side of the sink, and feels the earth heave beneath her. Her sight pitches. The taste of her own tears no longer comforts her.

Daily she takes the bus down to the harbor; and in the breathing darkness at night, she dreams of drowning.

Questions for consideration

What is the role of fantasy in this story?

Is this a story of love?

About the story

For centuries on the coasts of Scotland and Ireland, people have told the stories of selkies: seals who shed their skins to become men and women on the land, who must have their sealskins to return to the sea. "I am a man upon the land, I am a selkie on the sea ..." Some say that they live like ordinary seals, and only come ashore in human shape to dance at the full moon; others tell of palaces beneath the waves, cities of coral and pearl, roofed with gold. Seal-men seduce human women and their children are ill-fated heroes. A hunter breaks his knife in the shoulder of a seal and years later finds the missing half-blade in the house of the stranger who saved him from drowning. Fishermen steal the skins of seal-women and bring them home as brides, bind them to dry land until they should find their skins—their true selves—and return to the ocean, abandoning husband, home, hearth, and children for their oldest and wildest love. "Skins on Sule Skerry" looks at this last motif from the perspective of the seal-woman brought ashore: in all ways trapped in a life that is not her own. The author likes to imagine that someday she will find her skin stashed in the attic and walk back into the sea. But it is the reader who has to decide how this story ends.

About the author

Sonya Taaffe has a confirmed addiction to myth, folklore, and dead languages. Her poem "Matlacihuatl's Gift" shared first place for the 2003 Rhysling Award, and a respectable amount of her short fiction and poetry was recently collected in "Postcards from the Province of Hyphens and Singing Innocence and Experience" (Prime Books). She is currently pursuing a Ph.D. in Classics at Yale University. Updates, reminiscences, and memory can be found at http://sovay.livejournal.com/.

Love

Beached

By Jessica Treat

She's taken the car he doesn't know where. She's gone off again. No, they don't have another car. No, he cannot say where and No, he does not think she will call, write a note retrospectively . . .

Why does she have to do this? Why is it so difficult to write out on a scrap of paper, tape it to the door: I've gone to—. I'll be back by—. Surely one can be spontaneous, feel free, but also keep one's partner informed? No, not possible. Quite impossible for her.

He makes himself a cup of coffee. Strong as he likes it, no milk or sugar. For all he knows, she's gone off to get herself a cappuccino somewhere. As if coffee tastes better in a public place than home-brewed in their kitchen.

There was that time they'd stopped at a local favorite for lunch—they were on vacation, a small town in New Brunswick—a lovely screen porch, tables with vases of flowers, but no, she chose the indoor part of the restaurant. He'd relented. But felt the need to ask: Why, on a beautiful summer day—?

She shrugged. "There are more people here."

Exactly. Just the reason for getting away.

Like when they'd arrive at the beach together, he'd immediately head down to the end, where few people sat, where a slow rivulet of water tricked down the rocks. But he could feel her at his side, not quite with him—tugging invisibly—in the other direction.

"What?" he asked.

"I thought we might sit over there, where the other people are—"

Is it a fatal flaw? That she is drawn to people and places, while he is pulled toward the removed, remote, the private, and—it seems to him—infinitely more beautiful.

It occurs to him that this is exactly what draws him to her: her own remoteness. "Other people I know might be bothered," he remembers telling her, early on in their relationship, a hike they'd taken somewhere—"by the fact that you go for such long periods without saying anything. It might unnerve them. It doesn't bother me though. I feel comfortable with that about you."

Yet he also saw how she could be with others: a certain volubility welled up inside her, a cascade of words—ones he hadn't been treated to in a good long while.

He wants to get in the car to drive to find her. Then remembers that she has it. The car.

He stands at the door, thinking he hears the rumble of its engine, far off, getting closer—

But no, it's nothing. A lawn mower or tractor working its slow progress toward him.

Questions for consideration

What is the main difference between the two characters?

Is this a story about communication? How so?

About the story

In the short-short story or flash fiction form, it is easier to concentrate on one moment in that conflict, perhaps a pivotal one. In my story, "Beached," the conflict ostensibly occurs when the husband realizes that his wife has taken their car, having left no indication as to where she went.
The problem is of course deeper than that. He and she are very different we learn in terms of sensibility: he, given to privacy, quiet, nature, and solitude; she to society: the bustle and sense of possibility that comes from other people: be they friends or strangers.
The husband in the story seems to realize this, though it only draws him to her more. Yet by the story's end we still do not know where the wife is or even if she will be coming back.
The husband recognizes his love for her; does she also love and desire him? The story does not answer that question; the reader is left to wonder.

About the author

Jessica Treat is the author of two story collections, "Not a Chance" (FC2, 2000) and "A Robber in the House" (Coffee House Press, 1993 & 2004), and is completing a third. Her stories and prose poems have appeared in numerous journals and anthologies. She is the recipient of a Connecticut Commission on the Arts Award and is an Associate Professor of English at Northwestern Connecticut Community College. More information can be found at: http://fc2.org/treat/treat.htm.

Love

Beer and Gunplay

By Neno Perrotta

The plan has always been this: Friday we drink the beer, Saturday we cook the chicken, and Sunday we shoot the guns. Except for an occasional holiday, abortion or act of God, Linda and I have been doing these things every weekend for almost three years.

The door slammed shut. It was Linda with the Budweiser and chicken. "How'd it go today?" I yelled over the stereo.

"Good," she yelled back. "I bought a case of Brown's Amber for tonight."

I didn't understand a word she was saying. I wanted to hear about Budweiser, or maybe Miller. "What the hell are you screaming about," I said.

"Brown's Amber," she said, after she turned down the music. "It's a micro-brew. It's something different."

Linda has the longest, reddest hair you can imagine. And her favorite things to wear are tight jeans and tight T-shirts. When she gets close to me I can hardly think. I can barely see the world around us. I never know what I'm going to say.

"Screw the Brown's Amber," I said. "For your sake, it better be twice as good as Bud. And it better go with chicken."

"I got salmon," she said. "And we can drink all the Brown's tonight because I bought wine for the fish." Then she sat on my lap.

I was pissed, but I still wanted to kiss her. I wanted her to remember what we were. I wanted to make her forget about Brown's Amber and New Age fish. But I couldn't. Somehow I had gotten a mouth full of Linda's hair.

She rolled off my lap and onto the sofa. She took her hair with her and my throat was clear.

"I cleaned the rifle and the .40 caliber," I told her. "Everything's ready for Sunday."

"Sunday?" she said. "Oh yeah, Sunday." By then she had her shirt off and her jeans around her ankles.

Questions for consideration

How is the relationship between the man and the woman changing?

What does it mean that the woman bought expensive beer, wine and salmon, instead of cheap beer and chicken?

About the story

"Beer and Gunplay" concerns a typical working class couple. The man is satisfied with his life's routines, while the woman desires new experiences. If they manage to stay together, it will be because of their strong physical attraction for each other. The question is whether a good physical relationship is enough to keep them, or any couple, together for long.

About the author

Neno Perrotta is 59 and unemployed. His passions are reading, cult movies and gardening. He has a B.A. in English Literature and is the author of a collection of short stories and poems titled "Not One Thing About Science," published by Shenango River Books and edited by poet Jeanne Mahon. Neno is a member of the Fallen City writer's workshop. If you like his stories and are interested in obtaining his book, try his web page at http://users.zoominternet.net/~fallencitywriters for further information. Neno also welcomes email at nperrotta1@netzero.net.

Love

The Illustrated Woman

By Pedro Ponce

This was during better times. She called with her itinerary, reciting airline and gate numbers, her voice edged with hunger. I vacuumed, scrubbed, and laundered, shopped for two at the grocery store.

I waited at the gate, bouquet in hand. Next to me, a man was listening to the radio. The volume on his headphones was so loud, I could hear Liz Phair comparing a lover to the explosion of a dying star.

She surprised me from behind and pressed her lips to my ear. We collected her bags and left the terminal. I splurged for a cab. While the driver cursed between lane changes, I could feel the rush of the chassis through her clenched thighs.

We were barely through the door when she led me to the bedroom. We fell together, a tangle of hair and tongues. The front of her jeans gave way to my fingers. She lifted her hips and slid them down. An unfamiliar mark appeared just above her hip bone.

What is that? I asked.

She smiled and gathered the hem of her sweater up with both hands. It's Chinese, she said. Do you like it?

I leaned closer. It was a symbol I recognized from bumper stickers and New Age bookstores. Two tailless fish—one black, one white—curled next to each other to form a circle.

I thought you hated needles.

I hate getting shots, she said. I've always wanted a tattoo.

The Illustrated Woman   By Pedro Ponce

She was drawn to its simplicity, centuries of wisdom inscribed on her skin. Two sides in opposition yet necessary to make a whole, discrete yet inseparable.

It made me think of you, she said. Besides, I didn't like any of the other designs. Can you imagine me with a sunflower on my ass?

What about my name? I said.

She wrestled me to the mattress, laughing. Silly, she said.

Later, I couldn't sleep. I got out of bed and sat by the window, watching her. Her legs kicked free of the sheets. With every breath, the shapes inked on her skin rose and fell, two halves and the indelible border between.

Questions for consideration

What is a tattoo?

How does the tattoo change their relationship?

About the story

Sustaining a relationship when one's partner is miles away is itself a fiction. One can call every day, or send text message—what have you—but for all the ways the distance can be bridged, these only reinforce the fact of the other's absence. And it's arguably worse when one manages to see each other; the everyday pleasures of being together are tempered with the awareness that this is only temporary.

"The Illustrated Woman" is about this kind of situation. It begins with the narrator's anticipation of seeing his girlfriend again after a long separation. This eager reunion is stalled when he notices something different—she has a tattoo. The tattoo is disturbing to him on several levels. It's not just that he thought she hated tattoos. The location of the tattoo provokes his possessiveness; someone—another man?—has touched her intimately. But the tattoo's symbolism is most apparent if one is familiar with Ray Bradbury's "The Illustrated Man." Bradbury's story is about a man marked with tattoos that predict the future. At the end of "The Illustrated Woman," the narrator has a vision of his future, sparked by ruminations on his girlfriend's tattoo. The "better times" of the opening line are not just when the narrator was happier. This is also a time when anyone could wait at the gate for a loved one's flight to arrive—before the United States became a Homeland.

About the author

Pedro Ponce teaches at St. Lawrence University in Canton, New York. His short fiction has been published previously in *Ploughshares*, *The Beacon Best of 2001*, *Vestal Review*, *DIAGRAM*, and other publications.

Love

Nebraska Men

By Sherrie Flick

In Nebraska men keep small colorful seashells in their mouths. When they speak, which isn't often, the soft roar of the ocean hums behind each word. In this way they are able to understand each distant coast. They are able to look across their long flat fields and imagine ships rocking slowly to port, see each grain ripening earnestly in the Midwestern sun, see time moving slowly in a line toward a very specific day.

The men stop and take their hats from their heads. They squint and whistle quiet tunes to songs they never knew. They smile. At night they ease their warm bodies into crisp white beds; they slowly rub their wives' backs. The men make soft circles with their rough hands and are gentle as winter wheat. Just as the women are about to sleep, they say goodnight to them; they kiss them gently.

When they wake, the men smile and say good morning to no one in particular, to their sleeping wives' tousled hair, to the mist clearing. They are quiet as they get out of bed, walk down their stairs. Nebraska men understand three a.m. and cows. It is their job.

When they get thirsty, they shift the shells to a soft hollow pocket that has formed in their cheeks. This gesture makes the smallest noise, barely audible over the whimper of a dog, the leaves on a cottonwood. The men turn on the faucet that is beside their sturdy graying barn. The water streams out in a high screech; they tilt their heads, stretch their thick red tongues.

Love

It is then that the men come face to face with every single day in the year. They think how the one they're living today is no better than the last, how the next could possibly be the best one of all.

Questions for consideration

Is this a realistic story?

Setting is important to this story. How far is Nebraska from the ocean?

About the story

"Nebraska Men" is one in a series of short stories in which Sherrie Flick captures the culture and personality of a place by using a type of ironic magic realism. In Nebraska, men don't actually keep seashells in their mouths, but many of the rural farmers do speak slowly and thoughtfully. The seashells become a delicate metaphor to demonstrate the farmers' dialect. Also, the many fields of grain planted in this state ripple and wave like the ocean, and in this way the seashell reference connects the farmers to their own kind of ocean.

About the author

Sherrie Flick is author of the award-winning flash fiction chapbook "I Call

This Flirting" (Flume Press, 2004). Numerous literary journals have published her work, including *North American Review*, *Prairie Schooner*, *Puerto del Sol*, and *Quick Fiction*. Anthologies include "Sudden Fiction: The Mammoth Book of Minuscule Fiction" (Mammoth Press, 2003), "Flash Fiction Forward" (W.W. Norton, 2006), and "New Sudden Fiction" (W. W. Norton, 2006). She lives in Pittsburgh, Pennsylvania where she is co-founder and artistic director of the Gist Street Reading Series (www. giststreet. org).

Fantasy

How should a fantasy story be read differently than a realistic story?

Do you prefer to read fantasy stories or realistic stories? Why?

Can a fantasy story have as powerful a meaning for the reader as a realistic story? Why or why not?

Fantasy

And Counting

By Mark Budman

100 seconds. All your life you dream of free flight, but the weight in your chest holds you down.

80 seconds. A flight attendant finally falls. You don't know how she managed to remain standing for so long with her hands tied behind her back. Her skirt rides up; her thighs are skinny. Blood flows down her chin from the deep cut on her cheek. You want to pray, but you forgot the words. You want to cry, but you have no tears. You want to be tiny, like a fly. Or maybe big, like a fire-breathing monster.

60 seconds. The plane rattles. The pilot is an amateur, after all. The overhead compartments spill canvas bags and crocodile briefcases. A man across the aisle clutches his chest. A boy behind you says, "Mommy, mommy what does Allah mean?"

40 seconds. A woman next to you screams. You feel the air sucked out of your ears.

20 seconds. You hug her and whisper, "Don't cry, angel. We are immortal." She sobs on your shoulder.

0 seconds. The weight is gone. You are reaching for the sun; you no longer need to blink. Finally, you are in free flight.

Fantasy

Questions for consideration

What does it mean that the pilot is "an amateur"?

What happens at the end of the story?

About the story

"And Counting" is a magic realism (which is a genre of carefully realistic depiction of imaginary scenes and fantastic images) tale about passengers about to die on a highjacked plane. Yet the story is optimistic, hinting at the possibility that a human soul does not disappear after death.

About the author

Mark Budman's fiction, creative non-fiction and poetry have appeared or are scheduled to appear in such literary magazines as *Mississippi Review, Virginia Quarterly, Exquisite Corpse, Iowa Review, McSweeney's, Cafe Irreal, Another Chicago, The Bloomsbury Review, The Cincinnati Review and Night Train*. *Exquisite Corpse* nominated him for the XXVI Pushcart Prize. He is the publisher of a flash fiction magazine *Vestal Review*, http://www.vestalreview.net, and the recipient of the Broome Country Art Council grant. One of his stories has been accepted for the new WW Norton anthology "Flash Fiction Forward."

Fantasy

Snapdragons

By Alex Irvine

What happened next was . . . well, no . . . The night before, I was out on the front porch with a beer trying to look at the sky, one of those nights when the stars . . . the moon and Venus together looked like the Turkish flag. There was a garden tool of some kind, a trowel, I remember thinking, on the steps, and it reminded me that I'd told her I would water the snapdragons. But the mint, the damn mint was growing everywhere, and the snapdragons had been dead for weeks.

I traded in the Buick for that truck, and four thousand bucks, all for a hundred thousand more miles and a ride like a hay wagon. But this is America, right, and if you can't throw away money on a truck . . . I loved that truck. It was blue except where it was rusty, and it pulled hard to the left when you hit the brakes, and the four-wheel drive ground like a nightmare, but I loved it. On the fire roads with her, ponderosa pines and sun-warmed granite. I thought it would be good luck.

The doctor appointment was at three o'clock. We got up early, and I looked up where the sliver of moon had crooked toward Venus. There were high cirrus clouds. No, wait, the snapdragons weren't dead yet. That was when she asked me to water them. That morning. I was thinking, Which flag was it, the one with the moon and the star, or was it really Venus on the flag?

Water the snapdragons, okay? she said from inside. I was having coffee, and there were high cirrus clouds.

Yeah, I said, and stood there instead listening to her move around in the living room. She picked up this and that. Nervous. We'd been trying for a long time. I was optimistic about this doctor. We were optimistic.

No, I couldn't have remembered telling her I'd water the snapdragons. That was the night before. Later I went and looked up what the thing was, the garden tool on the steps. It wasn't a trowel. I had meant to ask her, but I forgot. So no, I hadn't told her I'd water the snapdragons. That was after I first saw the thing on the steps. But it was still there when she said, Water the snapdragons, okay? I think that's why I forgot to ask her what it was.

It was my idea to take the truck. Good luck, I thought. The grinding was in the clutch, not the four-wheel drive, and if I'd paid attention when my dad told me about cars I'd have known. Anyway it kicked out of gear on Alameda and I jumped a little. We'd been trying for a long time. I was optimistic about this doctor. I was nervous, and I hit the brakes a little hard. We couldn't have crossed the center line that much.

The snapdragons hung on for a long time. Longer than I would have thought.

Questions for consideration

What is the unspoken tragedy at the center of this story?

Why does the man not water the flowers?

Snapdragons By Alex Irvine

About the story

"Snapdragons" was the author's attempt to replicate the consciousness of a man so stunned and disoriented by grief that he is no longer able to put his memories in any kind of reliable order. The trauma at the center of the story is so immense that he finds himself circling around it, unable to address it, even as he obsessively goes over the events that led up to it. Through this manner of telling the story, Irvine was hoping to get a clear picture of the event itself across, while at the same time using the compressed form to give the reader a sense of the power of the tragedy to disorder his mind.

About the author

Alex Irvine has written five novels, including "The Narrows and A Scattering of Jades." His short fiction is collected in "Unintended Consequences and Pictures from an Expedition." He is an assistant professor of English at the University of Maine, and divides his time between Orono, Maine, and New York City.

Fantasy

The Bookkeeper's Treasure

By Candi Chu

Just another Arabian night, a spice of emeralds and rubies too bright for the three-piece suit that grays him. He spots Aladdin's lamp, disguised as a gravy boat on the buffet table at the office party, but when he bends to speak to the genie, he is nudged along by a hungry co-worker and his wish becomes lost like the moon in the morning.

With fingertips callused from years of tapping calculators, he touches a centerpiece rose to see if it's real or fake. He bends to the vase and inhales; a caravan of camels beats across the sand, the sun warms his thinning hair, the gritty wind whispers under his tie and over his heart.

The new girl from Accounting arrives late. When he sees her, the familiar beauty of numbers is balanced by the stranger, Scheherazade. She drifts through the cigarette clouds, a comet crossing the desert, shredding ribbons of gossip. He offers her his chair and the magic carpet miracle begins.

Questions for consideration

Who are the characters Aladdin and Scheherezade?

What are the Arabian Nights stories?

About the story

"The Bookkeeper's Treasure" tells the story of an ordinary man who longs for extraordinary adventure. While going about his everyday activities he begins to realize that his life is filled to overflowing with the components of a great life: beauty, hope, love. As a bookkeeper, this man's job is to count his boss's treasure, the company's profits. As a human being, though, this man's job is to be alive to his own treasure, to be awake to what is remarkable about his personal experience. His story asks each of us to take a deeper look at the magnificence of each moment, to discover the simple yet profound treasures we each possess in abundance.

About the author

Candi Chu is a writer/musician with a master's degree in Jazz/Composition and has worked as musical director for off-Broadway productions. An avid golfer, she lives in New York and loves to travel.

Fantasy

The House and the Homeowner

By Dan Leone

The homeowner found to his surprise that the home would not be owned.

"But I *paid* for you," he argued. He produced papers. "I *worked*," he said. "I went to work, every day, and I hated my job. See?" he said, as the house perused the papers.

"Mortgage. Investment. Equity."

The house just laughed. "What are these sheets of paper to my four-by-eight posts, to my beams and joists and two-by-four studs? What's your investment to my concrete foundation, your so-called equity to my earthquake retrofit?"

"Right, right, but I *paid* for that retrofit," the homeowner protested. "Don't you understand? My children grew up in this house. This is the house they grew up in, see?"

"Roots," the house had to admit. But there was a twinkle in its upstairs windows.

"Exactly," the homeowner said, thinking he was getting somewhere. "Roots. The children."

The house coughed, clearing its closets. "But what," it asked, "are your children to my tree?"

"Tree?"

"The big one out front. Its roots have crawled around and under

The House and the Homeowner   By Dan Leone

me. Now it towers over both of us. It doesn't wave papers in my face, just shades me through the summer, and cries on my shoulder every fall. *You* own me? You *own* me? I fucking *contain* you, Sir Homeowner."

The homeowner slammed the door behind him and sat in his car in the driveway, fuming. He didn't go anywhere, just sat in the driver's seat, behind the wheel, just sitting there, looking at his house and at the tree. The tree had a thick, straight trunk and long, sturdy limbs. He'd made tree houses in trees like that when he was a kid. He'd loved to sit in them with a cold drink and a good book on a hot summer day.

He closed his eyes.

He smelled leather, cigarette smoke, and dried coffee spills, with milk. "I own you," he said to his car.

Questions for consideration

In some ways, *does* a house own a homeowner?

Why does the man go to his car?

About the story

"The House and the Homeowner": At a time when all of Leone's friends his age started buying houses and having families, his then-partner was pressuring him, and he was resistant. (Thus the "then.") Leone has always enjoyed the flexibility and relative freedom of renting, and it struck him that their once-bohemian friends were in one way enslaved by the sudden seriousness and responsibility of home ownership. Then that the idea of ownership itself was a fantasy. He wrote this story to illustrate that point of view to his partner, who loved the story but still wanted to buy a house.

Underneath all that, the Self, psychologically speaking, is of course classically represented in dreams, etc., by the image of a house or home or building. On this level, the story might be read as an allegory for the uprising of the Self, the whole being, including the inner shadow side, against the Persona, the part of us that exists only on paper, so to speak, visible to the world. Something like this was going on somewhere in Leone, too, when he wrote this, but he wasn't thinking about that at all.

About the author

Dan Leone writes a weekly humorous column about food and life for the *San Francisco Bay Guardian*. Leone has published two books, "The Meaning of Lunch" (Mammoth Press), and "Eat This, San Francisco" (Sasquatch), as well as numerous stories in literary magazines and anthologies.

Fantasy

Rapture

By Gayle Brandeis

The babysitter said the Rapture was coming, and it was coming now. "Sorry you'll be left behind, Jew boy," the babysitter said, even though his charge—namely me—was a girl. He unfolded himself from the couch where we had been watching *Let's Make a Deal*. A man in a lobster suit had just won a donkey, a real donkey hitched to a cart and wearing a sombrero. I wondered if the lobster man actually had to bring the donkey home. I wondered if the game show people taught him how to take care of it.

"Gotta go!" he said. "Gotta go to God!" He saluted me, clicked the heels of his white tennis shoes, and ran out of the door.

I watched him race past the bay window, his arms waving over his head, his face upturned, laughing, like he was running to catch a bus, a bus that was going to take him to the best summer camp ever.

I called my mom at the insurance office where she worked. "What's the Rapture?" I asked. The only place I knew the word from was a Blondie song; it was on the radio a lot those days. The way Blondie sang the word scared me—kind of slow and drawn out, like she was falling asleep. And then there was a weird part I didn't really understand about an alien eating cars. I hoped an alien wasn't going to come eat our Cutlass Ciera now that the Rapture was here.

"Is that Daniel reading the Bible to you again?" she asked.

"No," I said, even though he had read a freaky passage to me earlier that day about a lady riding a serpent.

"It's a Christian thing," she said. "At the end of the world, Jesus is going to come take all the Christians away or something like that."

"What happens to the rest of us?" I asked.

"We all die a fiery death, I guess. I have to go, Janie. Be good." She hung up. She hung up on me even though we were both about to die. The phone squawked and squawked. It sounded like when the Emergency Broadcast System blats on the radio for a tornado or a flood. When I set the phone in its cradle, the quiet was almost more alarming. I looked out the window. The street was completely empty. The leaves on the trees were completely still. All the Christians were probably gone already. The fireball was probably on its way.

On *Let's Make a Deal*, a woman in an angel costume chose what was behind door number three. It was a boat, a glittery blue powerboat. She climbed up into the powerboat and I could see the jeans under her white angel robes. I could see her white tennis shoes, too, just like Daniel's. Christian tennis shoes. And she waved to the camera and I knew she was waving at me, and I knew she was waving goodbye.

Questions for consideration

What is the Rapture, according to some Christians?

What does the angel in the last paragraph symbolize? Is it an ironic symbol?

About the story

The Rapture will supposedly take place right before the world ends; all true Christians will suddenly be whisked up to heaven. A friend once told Gayle Brandeis that when he was a boy, his babysitter used to warn him that the Rapture was going to take place any second. Her story, "Rapture", came out of her wondering what would have happened if a babysitter had told this to a young Jewish girl. She tried to capture the sense of disorientation that would come from such surreal "news".

About the author

Gayle Brandeis is the author of "Fruitflesh: Seeds of Inspiration for Women Who Write," "Dictionary Poems," and "The Book of Dead Bird," which won the Bellwether Prize for Fiction in Support of a Literature of Social Change. Her second novel, "Self Storage," will be published in 2007. She lives in Riverside, CA with her husband and two children. You can visit her at www.gaylebrandeis.com.

Fantasy

The Human Pyramid

By Neno J. Perrotta

These neighbors of mine are driving me nuts. At first it was only a matter of clothing, then it got out of hand.

The big woman, the one with short hair, walks around naked talking on a cordless phone. There're always at least four or five little kids hanging on her legs or tagging along. The ones over three, they're naked, too. Babies wear diapers, thank God.

And four ponies and a llama they keep inside an electric fence. That's where you can always find the other woman, the one that most of the time wears at least underwear. She trains the ponies. I can't even guess what she does with the llama.

I asked the mailman, "What's with those people over there? What's their story?"

"Circus, I'm guessing," he said. "But they both get unemployment checks and letters to the kids from all over the world."

"Yeah. Sure," I said. "A world-renowned, nude circus." And to be honest, I was thinking lesbians, too. But, since there were so many kids, I kept my mouth shut.

Now don't get me wrong. I've got nothing against nakedness. And I like kids and ponies as much as the next guy. It wasn't until a few weeks ago that the carnival-like goings on became too much for me. That's when they started with the human pyramids. To be specific, the naked-human pyramids.

The Human Pyramid   By Neno J. Perrotta

Every time they try, the whole thing comes crashing down. With those diapers on top it's a snow-capped mountain of naked flesh. It's a miracle no one ever gets hurt.

So, now I have to worry that they're not too bright. Hell, everyone knows you need at least one strong man to anchor a human pyramid. Maybe more.

That's what's driving me crazy. I even went over and asked them if they needed help. "I don't know about the nude business," I said. "But I could wear a bathing suit."

"Thanks," said the naked woman. "But, no thanks."

"How about a cape?" I said. "Tight shorts and a cape?"

"It's a family thing," said the "bra and panties" woman. "We're all in one, big happy family."

"Okay," I said. "But kids can get hurt. Somebody can get hurt."

"No we won't," yelled all the kids. "We never get hurt." They talked at the same time, like they'd been practicing since the day they were born.

When I turned to go home the kids laughed and ran to ride the ponies. I stopped and watched while some of them fell off and seemed to crack their heads on rocks. One of the babies tumbled onto the electric fence, laughing and delighted by the steam that danced up from her soggy diaper.

Questions for consideration

What is a human pyramid?

Despite strange appearances, are the neighbors a happy family?

Fantasy

About the story

"The Human Pyramid". The narrator in this story is of many minds concerning his odd neighbors. He is confused and possibly repulsed by their extraordinary lifestyle. At the same time, he is envious of their strong and independent family structure. Hopefully, that the narrator sees the children as being superhuman adds a hint of magic and mystery to this story.

About the author

Neno J. Perrotta is 59 and unemployed. His passions are reading, cult movies and gardening. He has a B. A. in English Literature and is the author of a collection of short stories and poems titled "Not One Thing About Science," published by Shenango River Books and edited by poet Jeanne Mahon. Neno is a member of the Fallen City writer's workshop. If you like his stories and are interested in obtaining his book, try his web page at http://users.zoominternet.net/~fallencitywriters for further information. Neno also welcomes email at nperrotta1@netzero.net.

Fantasy

The House Broods over Us

By Bruce Boston

i.

It was always the house with its crumbling eaves and weathered gables, its turrets and cupolas, its ornate fretwork and blank window eyes. It was the house with its sagging porticos and scattered trellises, the dark green vines trailing up the walls until their leaves turned sere and pale in the sun's heat.

It was always the house with its trenched history and ineradicable stains on the hardwood floors, vivid as birthmarks or faded as old scars.

ii.

I gathered the tools of the draftsman's trade with a serious intent, to learn the craft of the cartographer, to create a detailed map with a detailed legend, extensive and accurate, that would not only chart the limits of the house but give specific definition to its varied elaborations.

I set out to explore its multiple levels and seductive recesses, the shadow and substance of its rectilinear maze.

And you came with me in your wayward fashion, less than innocent and far from knowing, to share my explorations and test the dimensions of the world waiting beyond each wall.

iii.

We discovered hallways that led to nothing and others that turned back upon themselves. We entered rooms that were ordered and others in rank disarray.

You sat at a slender desk in a high drawing room that bathed your flesh in films of light. I paced beyond the carpet, dictating imaginary letters to composers and poets and heads of state.

We slept in a Victorian boudoir rich in its mock oriental decadence, the portraits of dead sinners gracing our walls.

When I cut my hand on a splintered balustrade, your lips closed on the single drop of blood that welled in the lines of my palm.

iv.

When you turned back, gathering up the ball of yarn you had cleverly unwound to mark our distracted passage, I ventured farther to uncover corridors and cul-de-sacs that recalled ones we had visited together, standing rooms and sitting rooms and those stripped bare of all decor.

Was it days or only hours that I wandered before you found me crouched against a wall, unable to speak beyond a thirst that filled my body to its pores?

v.

We have settled in the rooms we inhabit and we do not stray past their boundaries. We stay close by our hearth and our fire beneath a mantel lined with framed images of these same rooms.

Beyond us we can feel the house brooding through days of neglect, the accumulated dust sifting into its bones, the sun shadows and moon shadows crawling across deserted floors, the shame in its solitude as it waits for a step to cut the silence.

Questions for consideration

Why is the house brooding?

Is the house like a "haunted house" from horror movies?

About the story

"The House Broods over Us" is the tale of an individual who attempts too much and expects too much from life, and allows a single failure to defeat his life. There is an expression: "Once burnt, twice shy." For this character, once burnt becomes forever shy. The narrator's perceptions of the house at the end of the story are no more than a reflection of his own feelings.

About the author

Bruce Boston has received the Bram Stoker Award, a Pushcart Prize, the Asimov's Readers' Award, and the Grand Master Award of the Science Fiction Poetry Association. He is the author of forty books and chapbooks, including the novel "Stained Glass Rain" and the fiction collection "Masque of Dreams." Bruce lives in Ocala, Florida, with his wife, writer-artist Marge Simon. For more information, please visit his website: http://hometown.aol.com/bruboston.

Fantasy

The Curse of Fat Face

By Michael A. Arnzen

The kids called her fat face. And when she looked in the mirror, she saw they were right: her cheeks were as thick as thighs, her eyes pushed in plump like buttons pinching back the fabric of her overstuffed head.

She decided her face needed to diet. So she stopped feeding it attention.

She wore a scarf like a burka and hid behind sunglasses.

She avoided eye contact. Especially with mirrors.

She blinked. Often. She thought of this as a form of exercise, a way to melt away the cheek fat.

But mostly she just ground her teeth and did jaw exercises, which required many private conversations with herself at night, alone in a dark bedroom.

All this was much to the consternation of her mother, who listened intently at the door, trying unsuccessfully to make out the language.

Miraculously, the fat-faced girl reached her goal in just three weeks. The kids began leaving her alone, targeting other people's faces. Perhaps this was because she had become sallow and pale and scary.

Soon she found herself facially anorexic. Her button eyes now sank inside her cheeks like peach pits in empty pie pans. Her complexion waned; the black rings around her eyes triplicated concentrically. And her face fat was still there after all; she discovered it had simply moved

The Curse of Fat Face By Michael A. Arnzen

to other parts of her skull, as if the cellulite had displaced to places where she'd pay more attention to it. It now hung in hammocks of flab from her jaw line and neck, like the dangly skin beneath an octogenarian's biceps.

At least, that's how the poor girl saw it. In her mother's eyes, she was simply thin. A week later, her mother could take no more of her daughter's privacy and selfishness. She confronted her as she was gorging on *Cosmo* in the bathroom. The daughter confessed to spending sleepless nights with *Vogue*. She was bingeing on images of models between purges of attention, puking up pretty in ugly wet chunks. She knew she needed help and cried out to her mother.

But when they finally approached the hospital, racing in her mother's Cadillac, it was too late: mother went over a speed bump and her daughter's fat face fell right off the bone, sloughing down from her earlobes and chin and slurping into her lap before spilling on the floor of her mother's fine luxury car.

Before they covered her with a sheet, Mother thought she looked impeccable, like perfect teeth polished to the color of clean whitewall tires. When she returned home, she scooped her daughter's remaining skin off the floor mats and poured it into a shiny jar to place on her mantel. Everyone who visited was mesmerized by their reflection within its grotesque beauty.

Fat Face returned their gazes, feeding, pressing up against the glass a little more tightly with every passing day.

Question for consideration

How does this story satirize the search for bodily perfection?

About the story

"The curse of Fat Face" is an allegory for the self-loathing of a person who suffers from "anorexia" (the chronic disorder which causes a person who is highly conscious of body image to stop eating in a quest to lose weight). The "Fat Face" in the story is a monster that is given life by the anxieties and self-consciousness of the person who has it and is, literally, "starving for attention." The family relationship in the story drives home the idea that this monster is really created by multiple levels of society (youth culture, the family, the home) and not just one person's skewed self-image. Arnzen tries to use the grotesque and moments of horror in all his stories to call attention to the absurdity of human beliefs, fears, and assumptions.

About the author

Michael A. Arnzen has won multiple Bram Stoker Awards for his horror fiction and poetry. The book, "Horror Fiction: An Introduction", calls Arnzen "the master of minimalist horror" and his collection of one hundred flash fiction stories, "100 Jolts: Shockingly Short Stories" (Raw Dog Screaming Press, 2005), was published to much critical acclaim. Arnzen teaches Writing Popular Fiction at Seton Hill University near Pittsburgh, Pennsylvania. Visit him online at www.gorelets.com.

Fantasy

The Mouth

By Lincoln Michel

The mouth on the top of Franz's head has a diameter of six inches. His address is 606 Hinton Ave. The electricity tower next to his house is sixty feet tall. Franz is an accountant; he immerses himself in numbers and yet he has, so far, failed to figure out the significance of these repetitions.

The mouth can speak, but only German. The mouth is rude and gets Franz into trouble. After a grueling day of accounting, Franz steps into the elevator holding his briefcase neatly in front of his crotch. In the elevator is a shapely young woman in a blue power suit.

"*Du hast einen leistungsfähig arsch,*" says the mouth.

The red handprint stays there for twenty minutes.

Franz wears a black bowler hat on the top of his head, to cover the anomaly. It was his grandfather's. Franz sits on a park bench musing over his fate. It is mid-May and Franz is the only person wearing a bowler hat. Franz is an accountant, but if he were an artist perhaps he would be more optimistic about his fate, given the history of famous faces obscured by apples and white birds. Perhaps he would view himself as walking art, perhaps.

A small squirrel, not cautious due to years of hand-feeding in the park, crawls along Franz's shoulder and wanders under his hat. It does not re-emerge. Franz weeps silently.

Franz sits nervously crinkling the thin white paper of the doctor's table. The doctor prods with his tongue depressor.

"It's a tumor," he says definitively.

"A ... a tumor?"

"Yes, probably benign."

"Benign?! It just ate a squirrel."

"I meant it's not cancerous."

"Oh."

The mouth is learning some manners. Eating some particularly peppery salami, Franz sneezes.

"*Gesundheit*," says the mouth.

Still, to Franz, the situation is becoming unbearable. He lies in bed at night asking god, "why?" But god does not answer him. If only there were someone for him, some kindred soul. Some woman with an eight-inch ear fixed to her dainty head who would hold him in her arms and listen, listen.

Questions for consideration

Is this a surreal story?

Does it share a similar theme with "The Curse of Fat Face" concerning how people are insecure about their bodies?

About the story

Lincoln Michel's stories begin as images in his head. The image of a man hiding a gigantic mouth under his bowler hat was inspired by the art of

Belgian Surrealist René Magritte. Magritte's work features seemingly normal images twisted slightly and often eerily. Michel believes we all feel, at one time or another, that there is something slightly wrong with us. Deep down, "The Mouth" is about the shame we often have over our differences, the resulting loneliness we feel and our hope for understanding. And also how tasty squirrels are to monstrous tumors, of course.

About the author

Lincoln Michel is a young writer from the southern U.S. His flash fiction has appeared in journals such as *The Mississippi Review*, *Quick Fiction*, *Pindeldyboz* and *The Vestal Review*. He keeps an infrequently updated blog at http://lincolnmm.blogspot.com/.

Fantasy

Wrong

By Aimee Bender

When I saw the row of elephants crossing the road into the mouth of the very fat child, I knew I couldn't sit back anymore. I ran over and shook the child by its voluminous shoulders. Do you really think you're going to be happy being this huge? I yelled. I don't think so! Do you really think these elephants are going to sit quietly in your belly? I don't think so!

A gray trunk clung to the lip of the child's mouth, and then was sucked up and away into its cavernous throat. The child looked over at me, his eyes enormous circles, and swallowed. His face so happy, his belly trumpeting. It is miraculous, he said, and then his cheeks were drenched in tears.

Questions for consideration

Is the fat boy crying from happiness, or sadness?

Are we always aware of the consequences of our actions?

About the story

I think of "Wrong" as a kind of very short dream, the kinds that are in between longer dreams, but are unsettling so they stick around. I can't remember where I thought up the image for "Wrong" but it feels like there's something wrong in it, like that feeling when things are slightly off or unclear. Who is the kid? Who are the elephants? Why are they doing that? Why is the kid so happy? What does the kid know that the scared narrator doesn't? I can't really answer those questions, but trying to capture a feeling there is what I was trying to do.

About the author

Aimee Bender is the author of three books, most recently "Willful Creatures." She has been published in various magazines and journals, including GQ, Harper's, McSweeney's, and more. She lives in Los Angeles, and her website is www.flammableskirt.com.

Fantasy

Centerfold

By John Briggs

When her husband goes out for the evening, he leaves her, now seven months pregnant, at loose ends. She decides to clean out drawers. In the bottom drawer of his bureau she finds a several-months-old men's magazine. She opens to the "Dream Girl Centerfold." It's a nude photo of herself lying seductively on a beach.

Her legs stretch out in a V across the pages. Her elbows prop her up from the sand as she reclines in a pose that causes her pelvis to tilt out and her breasts to arch back a little unnaturally. She smiles fetchingly along her shoulder at the camera. Behind her a fat blue wave curls itself into a glassy tube about to shatter against the shore.

On the next double page this image repeats exactly, except for a red line beginning to show between her legs. On the next two pages the line turns into a dark a stain in the sand. On the following pages the stain grows larger. She is bleeding to death.

As she turns the pages, the provocative pose and her smile never change, but the stain reaches past her feet. Throughout, the wind blows, lifting the ends of her hair.

Eventually, elbows still propping her up, her head lolls at a grotesque angle and her body rots. Her skin turns to rags. The wind gusts her hair.

When the last of her flesh has disappeared, presumably picked off by gulls and ants, she remains as a skeleton propping herself up on the

Centerfold By John Briggs

beach with the waves arching over. At least the stain has vanished. Her bones gleam sleekly in the sunlight. The figure of her skeleton cuts a stylish composition against ocean and sky.

She doesn't exist on the magazine's last two pages. The beach looks pleasant and inviting. The waves strike a cool, clean blue.

Question for consideration

The woman is pregnant, a symbol of life. How does that contrast with the slowly increasing images of death in the magazine?

About the story

The woman in "Centerfold" is pregnant. Her pregnancy has brought a major change in her life and in her relationship with her husband. When life changes, we often have a feeling of "unreality." This feeling of unreality is expressed by the scene in which the wife opens the drawer of her husband's bureau and discovers one of his "men's magazines." Such magazines typically contain images of anonymous "other" women displayed for the secret pleasure of a male audience. In this case the magazine shows only naked images of the wife. The strange situation of the story suggests the psychological fears and uncertainties the wife has about her and her husband at this time in their life. The reader of "Centerfold" might want to ask, "What is real about our relationships, even our very close relationships such as husband and wife? What is the journey of our life in this world: are we each of us in some sense individuals posing and decomposing on a beach lapped by the waves of time and change?" Think also about the contemporary culture that gives birth to this story. It's a culture dominated by the images we make of each other, by a feeling of aloneness and yet of being "on display" for the other. Each of us is also that "other;" we are both audience and image, like this image of a woman naked, alone and dying on a vacation beach.

About the author

John Briggs is the author of "Trickster Tales," a collection of stories published by Fine Tooth Press (2004). He has had over 25 stories published in literary magazines and chapbooks. He is the author and co-author of several nonfiction books on aesthetics and physics, including "Fractals, the Patterns of Chaos" (Simon & Schuster); "Fire in the Crucible" (St. Martin's Press); "Seven Life Lessons of Chaos" (HarperCollins), and "Turbulent Mirror" (HarperCollins), as well as "Metaphor, the Logic of Poetry" (Pace University Press). He is the senior editor of *Connecticut Review* and a Distinguished CSU Professor at Western Connecticut State University in Danbury, and co-founder of the MFA program in Professional Writing.

Foreign Lands

How can traveling to new places change people?
Is "home" ever quite the same once
we have experienced new places?
How important is language to understanding
unknown people and cultures?

Foreign Lands

Divadlo

By David Fromm

In Prague, in winter, the sky hangs low and smells of coal. Older people walk downtown with kerchiefs across their mouths like bandits. Younger people make out heavily on subway escalators, hands under skirts as they descend.

I am invisible. It is great and harrowing to be invisible.

The streets are made of cobblestones. Car tires sound like rain on a tent. Some days I don't speak to anyone, just walk around, taking pictures of things. Ride the subway out to Andel, where the walls are covered with Soviet-era murals. Big men with scythes and women in wheat fields. Skulk across Kampa Island, tell the snapping black-billed swans I'll be back after I learn the Czech word for bread.

It's *chleb*. Don't tell the swans.

There is a girl, but she is gone home to Gulfport, to its sticky heat and rising rivers. We won't meet again, because I am invisible. I have a heavy coat, and it has a hood.

Stare Mesto is the old town, full of old people. They are invisible, too. Invisible people can see each other. At the theatre, I get off the tram and spot one. A babushka. She has got her back to me. She is peering around the corner of a building, looking down the sidewalk for some unseen hand. I have learned the Czech word for theatre: it is *divadlo*.

Foreign Lands

This is a picture I will send to my girl back in Gulfport, the picture of the old woman peeking around a corner. It will make her smile, maybe.

I walk down the street, passing the old woman. She is clucking softly to herself. At the corner, I duck behind and affix the telephoto lens to my camera. In it, the street condenses. Things move fast, washing across the lens. I find the old woman in the viewfinder. Half her face around the corner, eyes cloudy with dementia. Searching the careless street for ghosts. Then she looks right at me, and smiles, and sees one.

Questions for consideration

How do we know the narrator feels like a stranger?

What has happened to his girlfriend?

About the story

"Divadlo" is a very short story that recounts the detachment of a young American far from home. As he wanders around a foreign city, he observes the people who live there but avoids reaching out to them. Then one reaches out to him. David Fromm based "Divadlo" on a real interaction he had with an old woman while living in Prague. The story reveals the contexts each person brings with them to such interactions, especially in a multi-cultural setting where language and history are reduced to the elemental.

About the author

David Fromm is an attorney in California and the author of *Away Games*, a memoir about playing basketball in the Czech Republic. He writes fiction in his spare time.

Foreign Lands

On Holiday

By Chauna Craig

"Stay away from your future," I warned one last time, but Agata only laughed and pushed open the glass door to Madame Elaine's. Her scarf wagged like the pink-striped tail of an invented animal, and she disappeared into a room I imagined full of candles and incense and curious cold.

We were on holiday, delicious days where our life together was reborn each morning. Our choice in restaurants was unsullied by memories of surly waiters or wilted greens. Our strolls took us to streets with unfamiliar names. We could always get lost, and we agreed we wanted it that way. We were mayflies. Living, dying, hatching again, our minds lighting softly on every sensation—the song of the street vendor's cry, the smell of roast lamb, the brilliant neon nights—then flitting on. On holiday there were no children, no resentful mother-in-law watching them and wishing divorce would triumph over reconciliation, no failed affair with a sad woman who tasted of almonds and will never open her door again.

On holiday there can be no regrets because there is no past, and there should not be a future.

I tried to explain that to Agata when her eyes glowed with the promises on Madame Elaine's hand-painted sign: *Psychic Readings! Your Future . . . Today!* But she checked the bills in her wallet and said with an even smile I couldn't quite trust, "This has nothing to do with you."

"It's a waste," I called. "A risk."

On Holiday By Chauna Craig

I waited on a sidewalk scuffed by the soles of a million shoes and marveled over everyone who'd taken this same path. Chewed purple bubble gum hugged the concrete, but I didn't pry it up. I waited. And when my wife returned, she started to walk, with purpose. Her heels skirted the gum.

"What did she say?" I hurried to catch up.

"It's a secret." She called over her shoulder and her voice sounded years away. I walked even faster and my calves burned.

"Where are we going?"

She stopped. She studied the street signs. She studied me as if trying to look into my mind. Finally she pointed east where the brownstones huddled in the shadows of early evening. We'd eaten Mexican on that block. We'd liked nothing but the margaritas and the appetizing chips.

"But we've already been there," I complained, seeking another way.

Agata shrugged and walked on, confident of her direction, expecting I would follow or get lost on my own.

Questions for consideration

Why is "On Holiday" an ironic title?

Would it be a blessing or a curse to know the future?

About the story

In "On Holiday," a couple attempts to look into the future with the help of a psychic reader, but the result is as unpredictable as the future itself. Vacations are a time of relaxation, but that doesn't mean a person's problems and concerns disappear. Sometimes, the holiday can lead to new, unforeseen problems.

About the author

Chauna Craig is a professor of creative writing at Indiana University of Pennsylvania. Her stories have appeared in numerous literary magazines and anthologies, including "Sudden Stories: A Mammoth Anthology of Miniscule Fiction." Her work has also been cited in "Best American Essays" and the "Pushcart Prize" anthology.

Foreign Lands

Gatwick Blues

By Kay Sexton

"So . . ." he folded his coat over his arm, picked up his case and began to walk towards the departure gates.

"So?" She felt like sticking out a foot to trip him up but he was already past, moving too fast, as he always had. "Is that it?"

"Janie," he turned, sweet reason in a suit and tie. "I'll be back in two days—we can talk then." He was gone, neatly side-stepping the bags on the floor, neatly side-stepping her fears.

As he descended the spiral ramp past the conical water feature that was meant to calm passengers, she noticed he had dandruff on the collar of his chalk-stripe suit. Good, she thought.

With the detached observation that airports often bring, she watched other passengers descend. A small Chinese-looking woman with long airbrushed fingernails and an Armani suit seemed too perfect to be real. The flight attendant could probably fold her into a luggage locker and she'd still come out looking immaculate at the other end. Janie had never been like that—she had hair that stuck out and shoes that were scuffed or run over at the back. Would Rob have taken her worries more seriously if she had been better groomed?

Two teenage Australian backpackers chatted down the ramp, tie-dyed T-shirts flapping in synchrony with their mouths. In her gap year, she'd worked in a local crèche. Rob had traveled to Switzerland to study canton politics in his. She wished she'd gone farther, done more.

Foreign Lands

Another businessman dropping into the depths of the airport—like Rob, but twenty years on. Silver hair, platinum Rolex, red congested features. He was a Type A personality waiting to drop dead. Janie had a sudden vindictive hope he'd do it on Rob's flight. He turned, sketching a wave, and Janie turned too, wondering whom he'd left behind.

She saw the pneumatic cleavage and blonde highlights of a trophy wife—or maybe a mistress—who waved back, but allowed herself a disgusted grimace as soon as the man was out of sight. Right, thought Janie, that's it. If it wasn't an omen, it was at least a warning. She pulled out her mobile and rang the Marie Stopes clinic. "I want a termination," she said clearly, causing heads to turn all across the departure lounge. "In the next two days, if possible. It's ..." she paused, wondering how to express her sudden loathing for her life. She looked out at the grey sky, punctuated by clumsy jet airplanes.

"It's convenient timing," she said.

Questions for consideration

What is the woman calling to "terminate" at the end of the story?

How do we know that she is unhappy?

About the story

This story was written as a result of ten years spent traveling the world. When a person spends a lot of time in airports, they become sensitized to the behavior of people around them. It becomes easy to spot the emotions that other travelers are trying to conceal and to guess their stories.

About the author

Pushcart-nominated **Kay Sexton** is an Associate Editor for *Night Train* journal. One of her short stories was a finalist in the 2006 SLS/St. Petersburg Annual Literary Contest judged by Margaret Atwood; Sarah Hall (The Electric Michelangelo) chose her as runner-up in the ESSP short story contest in 2005, and Kay was runner-up in the *Guardian* fiction contest judged by Dave Eggers in 2004. Her work is widely anthologized. Her website www.charybdis.freeserve.co.uk gives details of her copywriting and journalism; she blogs about writing fiction at http://writingneuroses.blogspot.com/ and has a regular column at www.moondance.org. Her current focus is "Green Thought in an Urban Shade," a collaboration with the painter Fion Gunn to explore and celebrate the parks and urban spaces of Beijing, Dublin, London and Paris in words and images. "Green Thought" has just finished showing at the National Botanic Gardens, Dublin, Ireland and is returning to London for an exhibition in May before moving to Paris.

Foreign Lands

The Lothario

By M. J. Rose

There were enough seats on the tram to Grinzing where the Heligenstadt House was so that Ethan and Giselle found two side by side. The seat facing Ethan was empty, but the one opposite Giselle was occupied by a woman in her sixties who held a small mirror in one hand and a tube of vermilion lipstick in her other. There was a slight indent and pale strip of skin on her left ring finger where a wedding band had dug into her flesh for perhaps forty years. But those years had not slowed her dexterity for applying makeup on a moving vehicle.

Ethan thought there was something odd about a woman of her age and obvious good breeding primping in a public place.

Under her black wool coat, she was dressed in a wine-colored dress and chantilly lace, the city's splendor echoing in the dress's frill and reserved charm.

Ethan stretched his legs and unconsciously put his feet up on the seat opposite him.

Entfernen Sie Ihre Füße *von dem Sitz!* The woman snapped at him. He noticed a glint of the future in her still-vibrant blue eyes.

No need to understand German to know what was being said. Giselle watched Ethan remove his feet from the seat and smiled at him. You just got a tongue lashing, she said. I take it you don't need a literal translation?

No, I got the point.

The trolley car creaked and swayed from the people coming on and getting off at the next stop. Although the public transport was on the honor system, people queued up to pay.

Ethan noticed the woman who sat diagonal to him had shifted so that now she looked out of the window, making an effort to avoid looking inside the trolley.

An elderly man carrying a small leather briefcase took the seat where Ethan had rested his feet. His hair and groomed handlebar mustache shone the silver of a Gustav Klimt painting.

The Frau opened her hands in her lap. Her palms told nothing of her years. They were fresh and young under a slight layer of perspiration.

Taking a monogrammed handkerchief from her purse, she held it as if waiting for something. Then the tram jerked forward and the hanky fluttered to the floor. Leaning forward, she seemed about to reach for it, but hesitated.

The gray-haired man picked it up, and with a flourish, offered the linen square back to the Frau.

She thanked him with practiced surprise.

Their eyes held. He smiled, tipped his hat deftly, stood, and exited.

Once more the tram started moving.

For a reason Ethan could not surmise, he put his feet back on the gentleman's now vacant seat.

The woman watched him, but this time said nothing as the tram continued on its way.

Questions for consideration

What is the "honor system" of paying?

Why does the woman drop her handkerchief?

About the story

A moment in time in Vienna on a sunny afternoon, inspired this short-short story. Rose's goal was to take what she saw on the tram and take it to another level, explore how much she could make out of the incident and give the reader a definite sense of place and character.

About the author

M. J. Rose (www.mjrose.com) is the internationally bestselling author of eight novels of psychological suspense and two nonfiction books. Her work is published in over twelve countries. She devotes part of her time creating creative marketing solutions for authors and runs the popular blogs, Buzz, Balls & Hype as well as *Backstory*.

Foreign Lands

What You Can Learn in a Bar

By Robert Reynolds

This German man is telling me about self-defense techniques. His pint has remained untouched at three-quarters full for ten minutes. Make to hit me in the face, he says, pointing to the middle of his glasses. I slowly move my fist toward his nose and he redirects my arm to the side, plants a mock punch to the cheekbone with his other hand. The stool creaks. These are things I teach, he says. I teach for twenty years, off and on. Give me your hand. I hold out my hand and he cradles my thumb between his thumb and forefinger, bounces the hand playfully up and down, taking its weight. To me it seems he has muscles in his fingers. The veins stick out in his forearm, which must be bigger than my biceps. His eyes are small, intense, staring at my hand, staring at me. If you can get hold of the hand, there is much you can do. He twists my arm in a way it shouldn't go and my whole body drifts toward the bar, a brief shock of pain registering in my elbow before he pulls it back. Or the other way. I slide off the stool and have to catch myself with my foot. He doesn't notice me wince, or maybe he does and he doesn't care. It's not about power, he says, it's about knowledge. What is it that he would have me know? Pain, perhaps. Or fear. To know what to do, how to move, he says. Redirect. Make a stabbing motion at my heart. I do what he says and he blocks my arm upward. Two legs of my stool leave the floor. Twenty years I teach

 *Foreign Lands*

this. I ask him, have you ever been in a situation where you've had to use this? He leans over for his pint, takes a long swallow. Once, years ago. I am at a metro in Hamburg, I walk through a tunnel and two guys come from behind me. One tries to push me down. The other has a knife. I am so surprised I cannot think. They want to steal my bag but I will not let them. All I can do is fight them off, push them away as best I can, keep trying to go forward. I run, I block, push, dodge. He jerks his head one way, makes wild arm movements. I have no control. If I fall down I know they kill me. This goes on for several minutes. Somehow I make it to the end of the tunnel, and I yell. Finally they take off. I make sure that never happen again. He takes another swallow of beer. He nods, as if agreeing with something I've said. He steps off his stool and motions with his hands. Stand up, he says. Now I teach you something, yes?

Question for consideration

Is the German man an expert at self-defense techniques? How do you know?

About the story

In "What You Can Learn in a Bar," two men are talking in a bar. The person telling the story is an American, the other man is a German who does not speak English very well. The German brags that he is a martial arts expert, someone who has taught self-defense techniques for twenty years. He is less interested in drinking his beer than in impressing the American with his

What You Can Learn in a Bar   By Robert Reynolds

knowledge of the martial arts. After the German twice demonstrates somewhat painfully a self-defense move, he says that successful self-defense has less to do with power than with knowledge. The American asks himself what kind of knowledge the German wants him to know. Does he want him to know about pain? About fear? The American asks the German if he ever had a chance to use his self-defense techniques. For the first time the German takes a drink of his beer. This suggests that what he is about to say is painful for him. The German then tells how he was attacked by thieves in a subway station in Germany years ago. This was the only time he might have used his self-defense tactics. What he communicates is that he felt powerless, vulnerable, and afraid that he was going to be killed. The German drinks more beer and asks the American to get out of his chair. He nods, the American thinks, as if agreeing with something he's said. This could refer back to the question the American asked himself about what the German might want him to know, something about fear or pain. The last line of the story could have a couple of different meanings. When the German says, "Now I teach you something, yes?" he is saying that he is going to show the American another self-defense maneuver. Because he has been somewhat aggressive, and because he has made himself feel weak or vulnerable by revealing an event in his past, he might make the American suffer for making him feel vulnerable. On a second level, saying "Now I teach you something, yes?" could refer to what the American (and the reader) might learn from the German's experience (and the story): That his studying and teaching martial arts for so long might have been his way to try to make up for his own feelings of fear and vulnerability. Perhaps causing pain to others is his own primitive way of wanting to make others feel what he has felt, something he has never entirely recovered from, something he's constantly on guard against.

This story does not use quotation marks to indicate dialogue, a technique that has been used more often in recent American writing. The lack of quotation marks can cause some confusion on first reading, but sometimes the effect produced is more interesting than the clear writing produced by the use of quotation marks.

About the author

Robert Reynolds' stories have appeared in *Vestal Review*, *Tampa Review*, and at www.mrbellersneighborhood.com. He is a former Contributing Editor and Contributing Associate, respectively, of the *Boston Book Review* and the *Harvard Review*. Currently he is working on a collection of stories and a memoir of shorts titled "Military Son." He lives in Austin, Texas.

Foreign Lands

La Luna de los Tres Limones

By Steve Frederick

A cluster of fruit dangled like three moons from the lemon tree outside my balcony. The real moon was nowhere to be seen, obscured by the thatched roof of the hotel, perhaps, or simply too low on the horizon to see.

Brassy mariachi rhythms blared from the town square below, rising fog-like through the turgid tropical air. I lit a Cuban cigar and watched the hips of the cleaning girl sway in time as she swept the stones of the plaza. The watchman had already swung shut the heavy gates, and I pulled the cork on the cheap cane rum I'd secured in the square during the heat of the day.

I had no ice, but with a slice of lemon I could manage to swill the stuff tequila-style. I speared a ripe fruit with my Buck knife and sectioned it neatly into eighths.

I couldn't make out the words, but it was clear the mariachis were yelping a bawdy lyric. The girl stepped livelier in the torchlight, lifting her skirts with one hand and swirling about the flagstones. By the time I finished the first lemon, the rum was seeping through my muscles like a tonic, and I ached to join her.

I plucked a second lemon and sliced it less precisely, then tossed aside the plastic cup and began drinking from the bottle. Deep in the shadows, I was unsure whether the girl was aware that I'd been watching her. If she was, she was being coy about it. She kicked off her sandals and loosened the braid in her hair, letting the knotted end whip at her buttocks. The humid night air and the rum brought beads of sweat to my forehead, and the music filled my veins like a slow-acting hallucinogen. I peeled off my shirt and let the breeze trace feathery hieroglyphs on my chest.

I drew deeply on the cigar, and she suddenly stopped and faced me. She drew a finger to her swollen lips and mocked me, her cheeks sucked inward as if she were drawing me in. I tipped the bottle back and swallowed deeply, grateful that my night had taken a promising turn. The girl laughed loudly and opened her buttons, jiggling her cleavage in my direction. I flicked the cigar butt aside and beckoned to her, and she opened her arms wide.

The music slowed to a dreamy waltz. Out of the shadows below me stepped the watchman, and she floated lightly into his arms. I watched in disbelief as they swayed to the slow, sinuous rhythm, both oblivious to the deluded fool in the shadows above. I plucked the third lemon and hurled it hard over the wall. A chattered curse answered from the street below, giving the lovers pause for a brief, distracted moment.

Questions for consideration

What is the narrator's delusion?

What does the Spanish title mean in English?

About the story

"La Luna de Los Tres Limones" is about intoxication, infatuation and self-delusion. The lemons are employed to mask the harshness of the alcohol, but they're effective only until their own bitterness intrudes. Throwing the third lemon relieves the narrator's frustration for a moment, but is far from a solution to his loneliness.

About the author

Steve Frederick is a Nebraska writer. "La Luna de los Tres Limones" was his first work of very short fiction.

War and Crime

Why are people fascinated with reading about crime and criminals?

What could cause an honest person to commit a crime?

How big a role does guilt play in our lives?

War and Crime

How Could a Mother?

By Bruce Holland Rogers

It's better doing this woman to woman, don't you think? Before we get started, is there anything you need? Do you want something to drink? Coffee? A soft drink? Do you need to use the bathroom?

How had the day gone, before all this started? Were you at home the entire day, both you and your boyfriend? Had your boyfriend been drinking? Had you been drinking? How much did he drink during the day? In the evening? And you? How much did you have? Can you estimate? More than a six-pack? More than two six-packs? Was your daughter in the house with you the whole time?

When was it that your daughter—when was it that Josie started to cry? What was your state of mind when you punished her? What were you thinking when she wouldn't stop crying? Did your boyfriend say anything about Josie's crying? What did he say? What did you do to make her stop? Then, what did your boyfriend do? Did you do anything to restrain him? Did you say anything? No, I mean, did you say anything to your boyfriend about what he was doing to your daughter?

Did you try to wake her up right away? Did you check her pulse? Did you listen for her breathing? When was the next time that you checked on her condition?

What time did you wake up? How soon after you woke up did you check on your daughter? You could tell right away? How did you know? Then what did you do? Was the abduction story his idea, or yours? Which car did you take? How did you come to choose Cascadia State Park? Had you been to the area before? When had he been there? Did he say anything to you about why he thought the park would be a good place? Where were you when you called the police to report her missing?

Is there anything you'd like to add?

Does this typescript accurately reflect what you have told me? Do you need more time to read it before you sign?

Can you guess how it feels for me, even with all the practice I have, to ask these questions? Do you wonder what questions I'm not able to ask you? Do you wonder if I have children of my own? Are you a monster? What is a monster? Did you know there were officers like me who handled only cases like this, one after another? Do you have any thoughts about the question no one can answer? Not the one everyone asks, but the one only a mother who has felt her own hands shake with a rage that is bigger than she is can ask? Not that I'd willingly trade the suffering on my side of the table for the suffering on your side, but why haven't I? Why not?

Questions for consideration

What crime has been committed?

What effect is created by telling the story in the form of questions, with the criminal mother never responding?

How Could a Mother?   By Bruce Holland Rogers   151

About the story

This is a challenging story because the reader must infer so much of it. "How Could a Mother?" is told in the form of questions. The person asking the questions is a female police officer. Most of the questions are actually things she says out loud to the criminal suspect who she is interrogating. However, the questions in the final paragraph are almost certainly things that the police officer wonders to herself but does not say aloud.

The story assumes that the suspect has already confessed to the crime. The police officer is interviewing her to obtain an accurate statement about the circumstances of the crime. "Drinking" of course means drinking alcohol. Beer is often sold in packages of six bottles or cans: a six-pack.

It is up to the reader to imagine, based on the police officer's questions, what the mother's answers must be. The question about "the abduction story" suggests that in an attempt to hide the girl's death, the mother and the mother's boyfriend must have told the authorities the lie that the girl had been kidnapped by a stranger. They hid the body first, and then called the police with their false report.

The title of the story is a shortening of a common question that people might ask when they hear about a mother behaving cruelly or irresponsibly to her own child. The entire question would be, "How could a mother do such a thing?" The assumption is that mothers never feel anything but tenderness or protectiveness toward their own children. But even very good parents may sometimes feel rage when, for example, a child cries and cries and cannot be comforted. Most parents feel such rage fleetingly and do not act on it in any violent way. But frustration and rage, no less than tenderness, can be as much a part of what parents sometimes feel. People all may feel a full range of emotions, good and bad, admirable and not. This is true both for the good parent and for the terrible mother in this story.

About the author

Bruce Holland Rogers is the author of four collections of stories, and he is especially well known for writing very, very short fiction. He lives in Eugene, Oregon, near the west coast of the U.S.A. Readers all over the world receive his stories by e-mail subscription: www.shortshortshort.com.

War and Crime

Three Soldiers

By Bruce Holland Rogers

1. The Hardest Question
My marines bring me questions. "When do we get to shower?" "Sergeant, how do you say 'Good afternoon' again?" "Sarge, where can I get more gun oil?"

I have answers. "Tomorrow, maybe." "*Maysuh alheer.*" "Use mine."

Answering their questions is my job. But when Anaya was shot and bleeding out, he grabbed my arm and said, "Sergeant? Sergeant?" I understood the question, but damn.

I didn't have an answer.

2. Foreign War
No U.S. soldier who could see that kid would have shot him. But that's long-range ordnance for you. Calder stood next to me in the street, looking at the pieces.

"We've come so far from home," he said, "that we'll never get back."

"You dumb-ass," I said. But a year later, I stood on the tarmac hugging my child, thinking of that kid in pieces, and I wasn't home.

3. Decisions, Decisions
In morning twilight far away, my men are making up their minds: What's that guy carrying?
Friend or foe?

War and Crime

I should be there, helping them decide. My wife and my parents do their best to make Christmas dinner conversation around my silence. An hour ago, I was yelling at Angie for turning on the damn news. My father, carving, won't meet my eyes. He says, "White meat, or dark?"

Question for consideration

What are the conflicts in this story?

About the story

Some readers have wondered if "Three Soldiers" is about three different events in the life of the same soldier or is about three different soldiers. I titled the story "Three Soldiers" to indicate that these are the war stories of three different men.

It is typical for a sergeant to take care of the daily concerns of lower-ranking soldiers, and the questions that most of the men ask are simple ones. One thing that might be confusing in this story is that I had all of the soldiers asking their questions at once, and gave all the answers afterwards.

"When do we get to shower?"
"Tomorrow, maybe."
"Sergeant, how do you say 'Good afternoon' [in Arabic]?"
"Maysuh alheer."

The phrase "to bleed out" has a very special meaning. Like the more formal word "exsanguinate," it suggests draining all the blood from the body. In other words, the soldier, Anaya, who has been shot, is bleeding to death.

Three Soldiers   By Bruce Holland Rogers

Exactly what question the dying man means to be asking when he says, "Sergeant? Sergeant?" is left to the imagination.

The word "ordnance" can refer to many kinds of military equipment, but "long-range ordnance" refers to bombs, artillery shells, or missiles that are fired from a great distance. It is unlikely that someone using such weapons can see in detail the destruction that he is causing.

When Calder speaks of having come "far from home," he means not geographic distance, but psychological distance.

"Dumb-ass" is an insulting word for a stupid person. It is a word that would be moderately offensive in most settings but is the kind of insult American men might use amongst other men without anyone taking serious offense. Among men, saying "You dumb-ass" can be a mildly rude way of saying, "I disagree with what you just said."

In the U. S., a turkey is commonly roasted as the main dish for the holiday feasts to Thanksgiving or Christmas. The breast meat is "white meat." The meat of the legs and thighs is "dark meat."

This story is an example of a fixed form called a three-six-nine. It consists of three stories, and each of those stories is exactly 69 words long.

About the author

Bruce Holland Rogers is the author of four collections of stories, and he is especially well known for writing very, very short fiction. He lives in Eugene, Oregon, near the west coast of the U. S. A. Readers all over the world receive his stories by e-mail subscription: www. shortshortshort. com.

War and Crime

Skin Deep

By Robert Boswell

Claude returns from the coffee house to find his suitcase splayed across the motel bed and the manager's wife picking through his shirts and underwear.

"Is this a scam?" He sets the cup of bitter coffee on the television. "Your husband sends me across the street while you rip me off?"

She shakes her head. "Nothing that fancy." Crossing her arms, she grips her shoulders: white blouse, frayed jeans, bare feet. A decade younger than her husband and as thin as a prayer. "Wondered what I could tell about you from your things." Her tongue lingers in the dark aperture between the rows of teeth. The face she shows him is narrow, pale, lovely. "Don't tell Teddy. He has a temper." Not long ago she shaved her head, the down a filter through which she must be seen. "I haven't taken anything." She extends her arms, standing cruciform. "Search me."

"Not necessary," Claude says.

"Frisk me."

"Forget it."

"You'll feel better if you're certain." Then she adds, "Close the door first."

"I don't need to search you." He closes the door.

"I'll shut my eyes."

Her clothing is tight, her bones the bones of a bird. She couldn't hide a matchbook. Claude runs his hands along her ribs and down her thighs. She remains in the windmill position. He pats against her back and buttocks. He presses against her small breasts. Finally he pushes her arms down, which causes her eyes to open, as if she were a mechanical doll.

"Satisfied?" she asks.

"What does my bag tell you about me?"

"You dress well. And you don't know yourself."

"I forgot to check here." He slips a finger inside the waist of her jeans, the gap between the denim and her pale skin. He paces a circle around her, rimming her pants with his finger. When he stands in front of her again, he lifts her shirt: small breasts, nipples upturned, fruit plucked prematurely from the vine.

"I guess you're clean," he says.

"Certain?"

He unbuttons her jeans, tugs them down. Her panties slide along her thighs, slanting and rippled like a flag. Her pubis is shaved to a narrow strip. His hand slides between her legs.

"You don't appear to be hiding anything."

She grips his hand and begins rocking her pelvis. "I can come like this." A drop of sweat forms beneath her fine hair, the scalp turning pink.

After, she says, "Watch me walk." She shuffles with her pants down to the bathroom. "You have to do yourself," she calls. "I'm a married woman." Her laughter's round, complicated, lovely to hear. She reappears, buttoning the jeans. "We have rules about what I should and shouldn't do."

"You should gain some weight," Claude says.

A veil descends. "I like myself this way." She slams the door twice before the latch clicks.

Claude slides the chain into its slot. He takes the paper cup from the television, the coffee still warm, still bitter and burnt, but easier to swallow.

Questions for consideration

What is a motel?

Why is the woman looking through Claude's suitcase?

About the story

"Skin Deep" is set in a cheap motor hotel, which is a favorite setting for American noir novels—a violent, sexy, and highly stylized crime genre. The story enacts a typical scene between the tough male lead and the sexy female (known in the genre as the "femme fatale") he encounters. However, this story makes the femme fatale an anorexic, which works against the expectations of the form.

About the author

Robert Boswell is the author of five novels ("Century's Son", "American Owned Love", "Mystery Ride", "The Geography of Desire", "Crooked Hearts"), two story collections ("Living to Be 100", "Dancing in the Movies"), and one play ("Tongues"). He shares the Cullen Chair in Creative Writing at the University of Houston with his wife, Antonya Nelson.

War and Crime

No Questions Asked

By Patrick Weekes

I'd had less than twenty bucks in it, and I'd cancelled the credit cards when I noticed it was gone. But it was a nice wallet, and I sorely missed the personal mementos—a few photos, a half-dollar that had always brought me luck, a particularly apt fortune cookie fortune. So I took out the ad:

"Lost Wallet—blk men's, l/s city library. Rwd if Ret—No Questions Asked."

One week later, I got the call.

"Are you certain?" A raspy voice, slow, stumbling, as though repeating syllables learned by rote.

"Absolutely. Twenty bucks, no questions."

"You swear to that? Promise, and I will come."

I did.

He was good as his word, the gangly, hunched-over man in the baggy brown coat. We met in the park. His eyes burned with a bloodshot ferocity. His gloved fingers thrust it upon me as though it burned him. He never spoke.

Now my wallet glows under ultraviolet light. Sometimes I see scales in the pattern of the black leather, or perhaps they are circles. At times, it suddenly burns, heavy with scorching urgency. Other times it is cold, afraid, burrowing into the recess of my pocket. Each time, I spin and search the crowd in the street around me, looking for a reason, a logic. I find nothing.

The fortune cookie fortune is subtly altered, the meaning different though the words are unchanged. The lucky numbers on the back now form the Fibbonacci Sequence. My lucky half-dollar shows the leering countenance of a man I do not recognize.

I cannot throw it away. I have tried, but always I must return, sifting frantically through the dumpster until my fingers bleed, until I find it. I put it in a lead-lined box when I go to sleep to avoid unnatural dreams, filled with words in a language I do not understand, though I have learned the syllables by rote.

I see him, the man in the baggy brown coat. I see him in the street, the subway, the library from time to time. He smiles at me, a rictus grin, and I glare or shudder as my pocket burns, grows heavy.

But I never ask.

After all, a promise is a promise.

Question for consideration

Why does the narrator feel different about his wallet after it is returned?

About the story

Weekes wrote "No Questions Asked" after his own wallet disappeared, and he put an ad in the paper noting that he would give a reward for its return, with no questions asked. His wallet never reappeared, but he wondered how strange things might happen to the wallet that would make him regret his promise not to ask any questions.

This formed the main goal of the story: the main character makes what he thinks is a simple promise, only to have the wallet be disturbing after its return. Weekes wants the wallet to be as strange as possible, so that the main character's decision to honor his promise comes off as insane, or at least humorous.

About the author

Patrick Weekes has published stories in *Amazing Stories, Realms of Fantasy, Strange Horizons*, and several anthologies and small-press magazines. He currently lives in Canada with his wife and son, where he writes video games by day and novels by night.